SIMPLE GOSPEL

THE MODERN OFFENSE OF THE CROSS

JOSHUA WEST

WESTBOW
PRESS®
A DIVISION OF THOMAS NELSON
& ZONDERVAN

Copyright © 2017 Joshua West.
Cover Art: Kiara West
Edited by: Norma Jean Lutz

All rights reserved. No part of this book may be used or reproduced by any means, graphic, electronic, or mechanical, including photocopying, recording, taping or by any information storage retrieval system without the written permission of the author except in the case of brief quotations embodied in critical articles and reviews.

THE HOLY BIBLE, NEW INTERNATIONAL VERSION®, NIV® Copyright © 1973, 1978, 1984, 2011 by Biblica, Inc.®
Used by permission. All rights reserved worldwide.

WestBow Press books may be ordered through booksellers or by contacting:

WestBow Press
A Division of Thomas Nelson & Zondervan
1663 Liberty Drive
Bloomington, IN 47403
www.westbowpress.com
1 (866) 928-1240

Because of the dynamic nature of the Internet, any web addresses or links contained in this book may have changed since publication and may no longer be valid. The views expressed in this work are solely those of the author and do not necessarily reflect the views of the publisher, and the publisher hereby disclaims any responsibility for them.

Any people depicted in stock imagery provided by Thinkstock are models, and such images are being used for illustrative purposes only.
Certain stock imagery © Thinkstock.

ISBN: 978-1-5127-7810-6 (sc)
ISBN: 978-1-5127-7811-3 (hc)
ISBN: 978-1-5127-7809-0 (e)

Library of Congress Control Number: 2017903372

Print information available on the last page.

WestBow Press rev. date: 03/07/2017

DEDICATED TO:

First and foremost, to the glory of my Lord and Savior Jesus Christ. All glory to the King. And to my beautiful wife, Kiara Belle. You are my inspiration, my partner, my anchor, and my love. Every day I thank God for the gift of you.

CONTENTS

Introduction ix

Chapter 1: Perspective 1

Chapter 2: The Gospel of Truth 13

Chapter 3: The Gospel of Love 28

Chapter 4: The Simple Gospel 38

Chapter 5: The Church 61

Chapter 6: The Prosperity Gospel 75

Chapter 7: The Offense of the Cross 94

Chapter 8: Overcoming the World Through Amazing Grace .. 106

Chapter 9: The Cross and Evangelism 113

For I am not ashamed of the gospel, because it is the power of God that brings salvation to everyone who believes: first to the Jew, then to the Gentile. For in the gospel the righteousness of God is revealed—a righteousness that is by faith from first to last, just as it is written: "The righteous will live by faith."

—Romans 1:16, 17

INTRODUCTION

It is with great humility and care that I take on the task of writing this book. It is only by God's grace that I am able to do so. I am not writing this book merely to write a book. I believe that I am obeying God's mandate as an evangelist to preach His true and full gospel to the best of my ability. I am a flawed human being and still in the sanctification process. I am sure that, just like anything touched by human hands, this work will be imperfect. I have approached writing this book from Scripture, prayer, and leading from the Holy Spirit, to the best of my ability. I have also let several pastors and Godly men and women whom I respect, read drafts of this book in an attempt to create accountability and clarity.

The only perfect book is the Bible and any good Christian book should get its truth from the Bible and draw its reader closer to the Scripture. If anything in this book, or any other book for that matter, is unable to reconcile itself to the words of Scripture it should be discounted. The Bible should be the proof text and the yardstick by which we compare everything.

Christian Inspiration

I enjoy being uplifted and encouraged as much as the next guy, but to the casual Christian book reader looking for another Christian inspirational writing, this is not it. I want this book to challenge you, make you think, make you examine yourself. I know I did those things as I was writing it. This book is centered around the Gospel of Jesus Christ and its rightful place as the central doctrine of the church. There are many things to study, many things we can talk about, many things that we can learn, but nothing as important as the gospel.

To the Scholar

You should know in advance I have taken great care to use as little philosophical and theological terminology as possible. I do explain theological concepts, but in order to be readable to a wider audience I've tried not to include academic terms except when necessary. If you don't think you'll get much out of this book because it lacks pretense and pomp, I would ask you to give it a chance. Sometimes the profound is found in simplicity. It is my desire that this book be concise and to the point. If you would like some heavier reading, I suggest, *City of God* by St. Augustine or *Mere Christianity* or *Abolition of Man* by C.S. Lewis. I have not set out to write something as weighty and deep as those works. I do not have the depth of Augustine, nor the intellect of Lewis. I am not a theologian, nor am I a scholar. But I am a humble student of the Bible and theology. I have also been anointed and called to preach the gospel of Jesus Christ my Lord and Savior. Although I purposefully refrain from being wordy, that in no way means that I have watered anything down. The truth is usually simple and easy to understand, although it is rarely easy to accept.

Simple Truths

I am not trying to reinvent the wheel; in fact, it is much more like I am trying to change a flat tire on a car. This book doesn't uncover new revelations about God. It asks the question "Where is the message of the cross in this generation?" It is simple, yet profound. Sound doctrine speaks about the sustaining value of the cross, but we fail to live it and preach it with the passion, focus, and care it deserves. Without the message of the cross, our churches are just buildings and everything we do in them is pointless. Yes, even our humanitarianism and social contributions are done in vain. This world is on a collision course with eternity, and everyone without Christ will be casualties unless we warn them. It is urgent and it is real.

Open Minds and Open Hearts

I pray as you read this book, and the Scriptures to go along with it, that you do so with an open mind and an open heart, not necessarily toward me but toward the Lord. Scripture should be able to change your mind about anything. If your mind isn't changing and growing as you study the Scripture, something is wrong. This is a process the Apostle Paul calls *renewing your mind*. Since we are born again into Christ our minds and hearts must be transformed as well. This can happen only through the power of the Holy Spirit and discipleship through God's Word.

> *Do not conform to the pattern of this world, but be transformed by the renewing of your mind. Then you will be able to test and approve what God's will is— His good, pleasing and perfect will.*
>
> —*Romans 12:2*

CHAPTER 1

PERSPECTIVE

The Christian that is bound by his own horizon, the church that that lives simply for itself, is bound to die a spiritual death and sink into stagnancy and corruption.

—A.B. Simpson

What you see depends not only on what you look at, but also on where you look from.

—James Deacon

But whatever were gains to me I now consider loss for the sake of Christ. What is more, I consider everything a loss because of the surpassing worth of knowing Christ Jesus my Lord, for whose sake I have lost all things. I consider them garbage, that I might gain Christ.

—Philippians 3:7, 8

We live in a modern world where technology moves so fast it is obsolete almost as fast as it arrives; where the possibilities of science and medicine seem limitless. Anything you want is available at the touch of a finger, or the click of a mouse. We live in the information age, and although we are drowning in knowledge, it seems we are starving for wisdom—wisdom that comes only from God.

Unfortunately, we live in an age where our culture's attitude toward the God of the Bible seems to be growing ever colder. Have we outgrown the old rugged cross and the simple Gospel of Christ? Are we so evolved and enlightened that our dependence on God is a thing of the past? It seems we have traded in the Gospel of Christ as being the only way to God, for a more modern gospel. Something not so absolute, something less black and white. Maybe something a little more relevant and up to date with the culture of our time.

Should we be adapting what we believe to fit in with an ever-changing world? Should we be careful to not offend the evolved sensibilities of this modern culture? The answer is a resounding no! Our world needs the truth. Unadulterated and uncut.

This world needs Jesus, the same Jesus that died on the cross and rose again on the third day. So why aren't we proclaiming the truth about the glory of this gospel from the rooftops? Why does is it seem we are retreating back from boldly proclaiming the truth about our Savior? The truth that without Christ we are destined for judgement and eternal separation from God. Where is the salt; where is the light? It seems we have cut out the salt for the sake of our diet, and we have dimmed the light so we can blend in and look like the world we were once trying to reach. Maybe if we fit in and look like the world, we can attract more people to our churches. Maybe if we tell people what they want to hear, we can reach more people. But what are we reaching them with? And what are we attracting them to? If we compromise the truth to make people feel more comfortable in our churches, we are doing them a great disservice.

If the Gospel of Christ is the only means by which we are

saved, then why does it seem many within the modern church wish to minimize its importance? They don't necessarily deny it, they just don't talk much about it—at least not *all* of it. They leave out essential elements such as *repentance*. Many people preach a "just-believe gospel," but the Bible clearly says that repentance is a necessary component of salvation.

> *Godly sorrow brings repentance that leads to salvation and leaves no regret, but worldly sorrow brings death.*
>
> *—2 Corinthians 7:10*

We say we want a real and meaningful relationship with God, but we can't seem to fit Him into our busy schedules. Our lives are cluttered with so much stuff we just don't have room for Him. So many things are fighting for our time and attention. In a well-meaning way we say with resolve, "I need to pray more, seek God more, fast more,"—as if it is work we have put off, or a list of chores we will eventually get around to doing.

I'm going to make a bold statement. We don't make it a priority because it's not a priority to us. But the solution isn't to buckle down and try harder. You can never try hard enough to make yourself love something you don't. Either you do or you don't.

Don't confuse what I'm saying. I'm not saying that love is a feeling, because it's not, but I am saying that our world is full of people who think that it is. They let their feelings lead them around, in and out of relationships, in and out of depression, never satisfied, without fidelity, without honesty. I am not talking just about people outside the church. There are many people who can never experience joy, because they don't understand what love truly is. Or should I say it this way: perhaps they don't have a genuine relationship with the one who is love—God.

> *Dear friends, let us love one another, for love comes from God. Everyone who loves has been born of God and knows God. Whoever does not love does not know God, because God is love.*
>
> —*1 John 4:8*

If we are not full of passion and love for God, it may be because we don't really know Him. We haven't pressed in enough to find out who He is; because to know Him is to love Him. It seems everyone knows *about* the God of the Bible, but many haven't taken the time to get to know Him from the Bible, from prayer, and from personal encounter. We form our opinion about Him from fragments and pieces we borrowed from other people's relationship with Him. You cannot have a proxy relationship with God, or anyone else for that matter. At least not one that is deep and intimate.

We are so overloaded with information and so busy, that making time for God is just another chore. Why do we settle for this? Why is it so hard to put the God who created us, the Savior who saved us, the Spirit that empowers us, first in our lives? Maybe it's because there is already someone in first place in our lives—us. Until we are willing to dethrone the king we have installed, we will not give rightful place to the King of Kings.

Now I know that most Christians would immediately agree with this statement on the surface, because we are conditioned to; but when examined more closely we find that many times people are regurgitating traditional, positional, and doctrinally correct responses without giving much thought to it. My question is this: where is the passion, where is the fire, where is the love? I love the church, and I love the lost, but those loves are just an overflow of the love I have for Jesus, because He first loved me.

PERSPECTIVE

We love because he first loved us.

—1 John 4:19

But God demonstrates his own love for us in this: While we were still sinners Christ died for us.

—Romans 5:8

The modern church tends to put the focus on us, the individual—our importance, our significance, our talents, our prosperity—focusing on these as gifts of the gospel, but the greatest gift of the gospel is Christ Himself. Realize that it is us who are to conform to the image of Christ, not the other way around. The reason why the church today is fractured, and its influence is ever decreasing, is because our version of the gospel has become extremely man-centered, instead of Christ-centered.

I love the church and believe it is God's platform for the gospel on the earth, but what are we using that platform for? The church shouldn't be a social club, or a place we go to be entertained. It should be a place where we worship God in Spirit and truth, a place where people repent of their sins and take on an entirely new life. The house of the Lord is where people become disciples—not consumers.

If, as the Scripture says, "everything is a loss compared to the surpassing glory of Christ," then why are we obsessed with promoting a gospel that is full of selfish ambition, self-worth seeking, and prosperity messages? Why do *we* need to be the center of attention? Why isn't marveling in the vast glory of God fulfilling enough for us? For one, we live in culture that tells us that we are the center of the universe, and what we want supersedes everything else. But it goes deeper than that. At its core it's our prideful hearts. It goes back to original sin. I don't mean Adam and Eve's original sin, I am talking about the fall of Lucifer. Lucifer became focused on himself, his beauty and his importance and wanted to share in God's glory. He felt like he deserved it. I'm going to say something that might ruffle some people's feathers, but God will never share His glory with anyone, ever. God is jealous for His glory.

Most church-going Christians would not openly say that they want to bring glory to themselves. It's one of those traditional, rehearsed responses. We know better than to say that, but if that were true, Christian bookstores wouldn't be full of books with strategies for personal gain, filled with methods and formulas to get what you want out of life. We would strive to bring glory to God and work to make disciples out of men. The best *you* is centered in Christ, His kingdom, and serving others, not you. Just like so many other things in this brave new Christian culture, we say one thing but our actions say another. The true Gospel of Christ is one of self-denial, sacrifice, and a cross.

> *Then He called the crowd to Him along with His disciples and said: Whoever wants to be my disciple must deny themselves and take up their cross and follow me. For whoever wants to save their life will lose it, but whoever loses their life for me and for the gospel will save it.*
>
> —Mark 8:34, 35

The point here is that God is not some cosmic power you can use to get what you want; the gospel isn't a strategy for success or worldly gain. He has no desire to empower your will. Christ is calling us to lay down our will, and yield to His will. What is God's will for your life?

I have been around the ministry for some years now and I can tell you that this is the most asked question I believe ministers encounter. What am I called to do? I can answer that question for every person anywhere on the planet reading this book. First, worship God in spirit and in truth; and second, continually conform to the image of His son Jesus Christ. But when people ask this question what they are really asking is this: where do I fit in, where should my self-worth come from, what part do I play? Self-worth seeking is a natural human behavior and I'm not saying it's not normal, but this journey should lead you to the foot of the cross. One of the roles of the church is to disciple young believers, and to help them realize that they should find their value in being a child of God, not in themselves. We should find our value and self-worth from Christ alone.

> *I know the plans I have for you says the Lord, plans to prosper you and not to harm you, to give you a hope and a future.*
>
> *—Jeremiah 29:11*

I'm not saying God doesn't want to bless us, or prosper us, because He does. And God does have a specific calling for your life, but none of these things should come first, or be what you find your value in. Your value in an ever-increasing way should come from the relationship you have with the sovereign Lord of the universe. It should come from the fact that He has made us sons and daughters, and that His love for us could never be contained. God does have plans for you and a will for you, but they are His, not yours. When you start to really understand God's love for you, and the lengths He was willing to go to save you, it should not only show you the love He has for you, but it should begin to make you love Him back. God's plans are always bigger and better than your plans, and any self-involved theology that tells you otherwise is wrong.

This brings it all back to love. Loving the Lord no matter what your circumstances. What if your role is not out front, or great in the eyes of the world? The question is, *Are you bringing glory to God wherever you find yourself*? We can try to cloak our selfish ambition in something noble, but are you striving to be great, or are you striving to bring glory to the one who is truly great.

Just like a ship traveling on the open sea, the places in which we get off base are subtle. It is normal because we are human beings, but getting slightly off course if not corrected, in time will take you far away from your intended destination. When I say things get off course, what I mean is this. Anytime any other subject, or doctrine, upstages the Gospel of Jesus Christ, something is wrong. It doesn't mean nothing else is important, but it does mean nothing else is *as* important. It is human nature to be concerned about our needs, and how things affect us and our families and our situations; however, unless these things are seen through the lens of the cross, we view them through an improper perspective, thus distorting their priority and place in our lives.

Without the Gospel of Jesus Christ nothing else matters. Nothing! Without Christ Jesus coming as a baby, living a life untouched by sin, being crucified on the cross, and being raised from the grave, every other doctrine, concept and teaching is lifeless and dead. People inside and outside of the church throw words around of so-called inspiration such as: hope, purpose, and faith, but unless these concepts are tethered to the cross, they might be well meaning, but they are meaningless, powerless, and empty.

The simplicity of the cross is beautiful, it only seems complex because our perception is clouded by so many different concepts fighting for space in our hearts and minds. At its core, it is simple. What makes it hard to accept is our preconceived notions and prior programing. As Christians, we are people who state that we believe and live by this truth, but what we state we believe and what our actions say is true, are often two different things. This is the line between what I call *Social Christians* and *Christ Followers* or *Disciples*. God didn't command us to get the most people to raise their hands in an altar service, He said go into the world and make disciples. What is the difference between social converts and disciples? Their actions. Although your actions cannot make you right with God, they do bear witness to your true belief that Christ has.

The question comes back to love. Do we love Christ more than anything else? Is the will of the Father our ultimate desire? In the American church the question is this: *Do we love Christ because of who He is or because of what He can do for us?* We are told that God wants to bless everything we do and our will is the focus. We preach and live a self-centered gospel and when things don't go our way we become bitter or angry or disillusioned, because we embrace a gospel that is centered around us, instead of centered in Christ alone. It seems much of the church today is in love with the world. They hope to somehow make peace with God, and at the same time do whatever they please.

This brings us back to perspective. How do you view your role in God's kingdom? Are you constantly talking about and focused on what God can do for you, or are you focused on what you can do for God and His kingdom? God already sacrificed everything He had to recover us. Seeing the cross through proper perspective should make you grateful, and your heart thankful, because of what He has done for you.

This is where worship begins—unashamed, heartfelt, loving, worship. This is why hymns of old are filled with songs thanking God for the cross; because there is nothing more touching and beautiful than the selfless and fiery love Christ displayed for us. His mind truly was on you and me when they beat Him and killed Him.

His eye was on the prize of the cross, His heart was full of passion for us. He pushed through pain, humiliation, torture, death, and separation from His Father, which was the most painful part of His entire ordeal. If you truly believe He did it, and that He did it for you, then where is the reverence, the passion, the love?

The true message of the cross is in short supply today. Self denial is not a popular message and yet we talk about the fact that Jesus died for us like we deserved it. Sometimes it seems we talk about it as if it is our birthright, or at least a human right, as if God owed us something. Many people seem to have entitlement issues today. We feel like we deserve something. Not just about the gospel and the cross, but as Americans we have a list of things we feel entitled to.

It is impossible to feel entitled and grateful at the same time. What makes the Gospel of Christ so beautiful and generous is the fact we have nothing to repay Him with for the gift He has given us, but still He freely gave. Through this, true perspective passion for the gospel is born. Sons and daughters sing the praises of the Father who gave His most precious gift to restore connection and relationship with us.

What is the ultimate purpose of the cross? Relationship. Everything God did was to re-establish relationship with lost humanity. Since Christ is the gift of the gospel, when we minimize the cross, we minimize Christ. The world at large doesn't have a problem with talking about a de-personified and vague God. A God without personality and without intention. That way you can make Him fit into your life however it is easiest and most convenient for you. As some kind of mystical force that sees and approves of whatever you do from a distance. Jesus shatters this myth. Jesus is God personified, the image of the invisible God, full of intention and truth.

PERSPECTIVE

The Son is the image of the invisible God, the firstborn over all creation. For in him all things were created: things in heaven and on earth, visible and invisible, whether thrones or powers or rulers or authorities; all things have been created through him and for him. He is before all things, and in him all things hold together. And he is the head of the body, the church; he is the beginning and the firstborn from among the dead, so that in everything he might have the supremacy. For God was pleased to have all his fullness dwell in him, and through him to reconcile to himself all things, whether things on earth or things in heaven, by making peace through his blood, shed on the cross.

—Colossians 1:15-20

Two of the most important points we can take away from that Scripture is this:

1. Jesus was present at creation which means He pre-dates time itself. This is important because it supports Jesus' claim to be God. Not only was He present at creation, but it says that "in Him all things were created." And not only by Him but it clearly says "all things have been created through Him and for Him." This should help us understand that our life is less about "our purpose," and more about being in "His purpose." All creation, including us, was created for Him.
2. Christ is supreme to everything and everyone. "He is the beginning and the firstborn from among the dead, so that in everything he might have the supremacy" (Col. 1:18). Christ is the head of the church and to be a sound and functioning part of His church, you are required to function where He

needs you, not where you want to be. He created you for that exact function, and in no other place will you ever find true contentment and joy as you will when you are in Christ's will, seeking to glorify Him, seeking to please Him, instead of trying to bring glory to yourself, and trying to please and satisfy yourself.

If the gospel truly is the centerpiece of our faith, why has it been marginalized and minimized? And why, when we do talk about it, we do it in a less-than-absolute way? What I mean is, in my opinion, it seems many parts of the modern church have shied away from putting statements about the issue of the cross in absolute terms. Statements like, "All things outside of Christ are subject to judgement." It appears that words like "judgement," are no longer okay to say. But without talking about His righteous judgement, we devalue God's grace and mercy.

We like to say it is through Christ we are saved; but if we are being saved, don't we have to be saved *from something*? Without talking about hell, judgement, and the consequence of sin, we sound absurd going around saying we are saved. Why are we being saved if there is nothing to be saved from? If there is no judgement, there is no need for salvation, and then Christ died for nothing

Until we see ourselves, our lives, and our place in this world, through the proper perspective in which Christ is supreme, that His death and resurrection was and is our only means of salvation, and that all things outside of Christ are subject to judgement, we will get everything else wrong. The gospel is not just a part of being a Christian among many other parts; it is *the piece* on which all the other parts hinge.

CHAPTER 2

THE GOSPEL OF TRUTH

Where I found truth, there I found my God, who is the truth itself.

—St. Augustine

It is easier to find a score of men wise enough to discover the truth than to find one intrepid enough, in the face of opposition, to stand up for it.

—A.A. Hodge

Jesus answered, "I am the way and the truth and the life. No one comes to the Father except through me. If you really know me, you will know my Father as well. From now on, you do know him and have seen him."

—John 14:6, 7

Have you ever wanted to convince someone you were being truthful, and to add value to your statement you said something like, "This is gospel truth." What are we appealing to when we add the word "gospel"? What is the precedent for such a statement? What value does the word "gospel" bring? Even people who do not consider themselves Christians use this word almost as if the word *gospel* and the word *truth* naturally go together.

The word "gospel" comes from a Greek word *euangelion*, which simply means "good news or happy tidings." This is where we get the word *evangel*, and the term *evangelism*. This is what most people would define as sharing the good news about Jesus Christ. Evangelists focus their entire ministry on sharing the Gospel of Jesus Christ. The gospel is the most important message we will ever share. It is the centerpiece around which every other piece of our faith fits, and without it everything else we hold to and believe, are meaningless.

Over time this term "gospel" has been so deeply associated with the life, death and resurrection of Jesus Christ that it is typically the first definition you see when you look in a dictionary.

Dictionary.com defines gospel as:

1. the teachings of Jesus and the apostles; the Christian revelation.
2. the story of Christ's life and teachings, especially as contained in the first four books of the New Testament, namely Matthew, Mark, Luke and John.
3. something regarded as true and implicitly believed.

The Gospel of Christ is a well-known concept, although what people actually understand about the truth of the gospel varies from person to person. Observers and bystanders have ideas about what the Gospel of Christ is; but what people think they know, based on fragments of information they have, and what is true are often different. As disciples of Christ, it is our job to share the Gospel of Christ to a lost and dying world, appealing to them by using the best standard of truth available to us—which is the Bible.

As the dictionary definition above shows, the concept of the

Gospel of Christ, and the concept of truth, are deeply connected. Jesus Himself is God in the flesh, and John 14:6 clearly states that Jesus Himself is the only way to the Father. Jesus Himself is the truth, and Jesus Himself is life. By this reasoning, anything that disagrees with the person, character, and teachings of Jesus, will not lead to God. Nor is it true, nor will it bring eternal life.

It is impossible to divorce the concept of truth from the person of Jesus. His life on earth was perfect and untouched by sin, true in intention and in action. The intellectual elect of His time tried to disprove Him and undermine Him but could not. Why? Because you cannot disprove truth. You can ignore it, you can deny it, but you cannot change it.

Have you ever heard the saying, *You don't have anything to worry about when the truth is on your side*? Jesus always had the truth on His side, and He still does. Jesus is truth personified. Everything He does is true merely because He does it; everything He says is truth merely because He says it.

Truth does not change, it changes things around it. The same can be said about Jesus, He never changes, but He does change whatever He comes in contact with. The truth is a rock that the sea of facts breaks itself upon. If the truth changes, then it wasn't the truth to start with. Facts can change. Facts are merely what we believe the truth to be based on the information we currently have. As we learn more about the truth of a situation, facts can change; but the truth will not change.

When we present the uncompromised truth about the Gospel of Jesus Christ, we have power to affect people—to change people and situations around us. But it is the power of Christ working through the Holy Spirit that changes things, not us. Through the power of the Holy Spirit, the gospel of truth changes what it comes in contact with. It shakes things up, makes things uncomfortable.

Uncomfortable? Wait you might say, that doesn't sound like the church I know, or the Jesus I know. Don't we want people to be comfortable in church? Never at the expense of the truth. If you are withholding the truth, or watering it down so people won't be offended, then woe to you. We are stewards of the truth, and it is not our place to alter it. We are not perfect, but to the best of our abilities we should deliver God's Word and preach it, uncensored.

We shouldn't try to make people comfortable in their sins. If someone is full of sin, and living contrary to the Lord, and they can come to a church week after week, month after month and never feel conviction, then maybe that church is preaching a watered-down, or false, gospel. If a person whose life is full of sin can come to a church week after week, and not feel conviction, but actually feels encouraged by the message, then something is very wrong. It's impossible for sin not to not experience conviction in the presence of God. The truth should bring conviction, and conviction should bring repentance, and from repentance we accept Christ and turn from our wicked ways. *Repentance*. There's a word that is not preached from many pulpits on Sunday morning anymore.

> *Repent, then, and turn to God, so your sins may be wiped out, that times of refreshing may come from the Lord.*
>
> —Acts 3:19

Repentance and faith can be thought of as two sides of the same coin. You hear a lot about faith in the church today but very little about repentance. The biblical definition of the word repent is, "to change one's mind." Many people say that repentance means to turn from your sin. That's part of it, but first we have to have a change of heart. When we fully accept Christ by faith, it is because something caused us to change our minds about sin and the road we are on.

Repentance is the key that separates us from those who merely *say* they have accepted Jesus. Our actions do not save us, but action is evidence that you truly believe Christ has.

> *In the same way, faith by itself, if not accompanied by action, is dead. But someone will say, You have faith: I have deeds. Show me your faith without deeds, and I will show you my faith by my deeds. You believe there is one God. Good! Even the demons believe that---and shudder.*
>
> —James 2:17-19

Your action shows by faith that you believe something to be true. Let's say I'm backing out my car from a parking place, and I ask my wife, who is sitting on the passenger's side, to look at the blind spot to see if any cars are coming. She tells me that no cars are coming and encourages me to go ahead and back out. I say that I believe her, but I never move the car.

That's a good example of "faith without works is dead." I can say that I believe what she said is true, but that is verified beyond a doubt only when I move the car. Churches are full of people who say they believe Jesus to be the truth, but their car has never left the parking spot.

> *Do not suppose that I have come to bring peace to the earth, I did not come to bring peace, but a sword.*
>
> —Matthew 10:34

The truth of the gospel, through the work of the Holy Spirit, should bring conviction to your heart like a sword cutting to the bone. In Scripture, the term *sword* refers to the Word of God. As Christians, we use God's Word as the standard of truth. This is the how we learn to live lives pleasing to God. We are directed by His Word, and empowered by His Spirit.

> *For the word of God is alive and active. Sharper than any double-edged sword, it penetrates even to dividing soul and spirit, joint and marrow; it judges the thoughts and attitudes of the heart.*
>
> —Hebrews 4:12

We need the word of truth to help us divide our intentions, because sin can deceive even Christians. When the Scripture talks about dividing the soul and the spirit, it is referring to the wants of our soul and the true needs known by our spirit. If the Spirit of the Lord is living in you, it knows what you need to fulfill God's will for your life and how to please God. Your soul, on the other hand, sees what's right in front of you, and gives desire to what you *think* you need. Sometimes your mind and your emotions tell you that you need something, but maybe it is something that will take you out of God's will, or will hurt you. Only through the power of the Spirit, and through the truth of God's Word, can we cut through the wants of the flesh.

This life we live "in Christ," is a life of self-denial. It means resisting the urges of our flesh, and submitting to the will of the Father, just like Jesus did. Doing what is easy, and doing what, is right is seldom the same thing. We must not rely on our body, mind, or emotions to direct us in our actions. We must rely on the Word and the Truth, both of which are the person of Jesus.

An immature Christian, or a Christian with an undeveloped relationship with the Lord, asks the question, "Is this right or wrong?" What they are really saying is, "Can I do this and get away with it and still be saved?"

A Christ follower, a person with a developed relationship with Christ, asks: "Does this please God? Will what I'm doing bring glory to His name?" This is a relationship built on love and caring.

When you understand what love and truth really are, you'll see that the relationship between love and truth are inseparable. God is love, and Jesus is the way, the truth, and the life. This is why the definition of love and truth are under attack. Removing fidelity from love, and saying truth is subjective, are not attacks merely on concepts, they are attacks on the person of Christ.

So many people are living the same way they were before they gave their lives to God—never growing in the fruit of the spirit. They don't have joy, peace, patience, and the other fruit of the spirit, because they missed the first one, which is love.

> *But the fruit of the Spirit is love, joy, peace, forbearance, kindness, goodness, faithfulness, gentleness and self control. Against such things there is no law.*
>
> *—Galatians 5:22, 23*

The gospel of truth is a gospel of love. God shows us He loves us in so many ways, but the deepest and most significant way is the passion displayed for us by giving us His one and only son to gain us as His children. When we accept His love for us, and reciprocate it by trusting in Him with our lives, this pleases the Lord. But the enemy of our soul, Satan, does not want us to love God. The one way he tries to damage our relationship with God is to discourage us from trusting Him, and Satan does this by attacking the truth.

He did this in the garden of Eden with Eve when he questioned what God had said to Eve. Eve told Satan that God said, "If we eat the fruit of the tree of the knowledge of good and evil we would surely die." Satan's response wasn't to attack God directly, but instead he attacked the truth using Eve's own desires.

"You will not surely die," Satan said. If Satan can discredit the truth, then he can discredit God. This devaluing of truth has continued on until this day. Satan wants us to think we can have right relationship with God without accepting the fullness of His truth, the Bible, which is His Word. Satan used Eve's own desires to make her doubt the truth of God. Satan always tries to make us question God's intentions. God will never trick us, never manipulate us, and never lie to us. His intentions are always good, and as true as His Word.

Christians cannot believe that truth is subjective, because the Bible is based on absolutes. The entire notion of right and wrong hangs in the balance of objectiveness. If truth is not objective, always the same, unchanging, then there is no right or wrong. This world wants to undermine truth so that they can live in their sin and feel okay about it. The gospel itself is the remedy for sin. Although God cannot be in the presence of sin, He was willing to sacrifice everything to be in a relationship with us. He found a way to redeem us and He gave everything to do it.

Only The Truth Can Set Us Free

Jesus is the truth. His words are true, he leads us in truth, his very being is truth. We are born as slaves to sin. Our minds, our hearts, our ways, and our very being is sinful. It's only through Jesus, who is the truth, that we are set free. Many people feel like they are right with God because they go to church, or because they feel that they are "good people." But by whose standard?

God's standard is perfection, which we could never live up to, because we are sinful by nature. Before we can ever be right with God through Christ, we have to accept the truth that we are incapable of having relationship with God without Christ. Our goodness by itself could never be enough. We are slaves to sin and the only way to be set free is to turn our lives over to Christ and be His disciples.

Being a disciple means that we center our lives around the teachings of Jesus. We follow His ways and not our own. We live our lives by His will, not what makes sense to us. If we understand it, and even when we don't, we will do our very best to obey Him.

> *To the Jews who had believed him, Jesus said, "If you hold to my teaching, you are really my disciples. Then you will know the truth, and the truth will set you free. They answered him, "We are Abraham's descendants and have never been slaves to anyone. How can say we shall be set free?*
>
> *Jesus replied, "Very truly I tell you, everyone who sins is a slave to sin, now a slave has no permanent place in the family, but a son belongs to it forever. So if the Son sets you free you are free indeed. I know that you are Abraham's descendants. Yet you are looking for a way to kill me because you have no room for my word.*
>
> —John 8:31-37

Jesus wants disciples. If we really are His disciples, we will follow His teachings, and we will honor His Word. So many people, even in the church, are not free. They are caught up in all sorts of sin and bondage, because they don't live by His teachings. We pick and choose the parts of Scripture that we can make fit around our lifestyle and our sin. If we don't like it we ignore it, and then we wonder why we are not free. We wonder why we are not living in victory. Obviously, we cannot live up to the standard of Christ in all His perfection; but by the power of the Holy Spirit, we can overcome the bondage of sin. Jesus paid the price and the Spirit gives power. We are directed by the word and empowered by the Spirit.

Jesus says something interesting in John 8:36, 37.

> *So if the Son sets you free you will be free indeed. I know you are Abraham's descendants. Yet you are looking for a way to kill me, because you have no room for my word.*

They wanted to kill the Truth because they were unwilling to make room for His word. They didn't accept the truth about Jesus and they were not willing to make room for His words, because it didn't fit in with their will and their ways.

The Jews in this Scripture, just like many people in the world today, think they are in right standing with God based on their flawed understanding—and misunderstanding—of truth. But in order to be set free by the truth, who in person is Christ, we have to make room for His Word which is contained in the Scriptures. We deny Christ when we deny His words, and we cannot be free from the bondage of sin, or be in right standing with God, until we make room for the truth that comes only from Christ.

> *Opponents must be gently instructed, in the hope that God will grant them repentance leading them to a knowledge of the truth.*
>
> —2 Timothy 2:25

The world doesn't need a more palatable version of the gospel, it needs the truth given in a loving way. If we don't stand behind entirety of Scripture as truth, then we will be ineffective as disciples and witnesses. It seems people are not all that interested in repentance, because to repent you have to admit something is wrong. We must repent of our sins and turn from our wicked ways, not just believe. When the Bible says *believe,* it means to trust in, to have faith in, to live your life by.

The church is saturated with a "just-believe" gospel. The Bible is clear that we must believe in our hearts and confess with our mouths that Jesus is Lord. But we also have to repent and turn from our wicked ways. The gospel should be preached with boldness, in its fullness, and with integrity and honesty. It's only good news if it is complete. We should never be fearful that we will offend people when we tell them what it really means to follow Christ. We should be more concerned with offending God than offending people. We will give an account one day of how we handled the truth, what we preached from our pulpits and how we presented the gospel to a lost and dying world.

> *Show me your ways, Lord, teach me your paths. Guide me in your truths and seek me, for you are God my Savior, and my hope is in you all day long.*
>
> —Psalms 25:5

The truth is beautiful and powerful. It cannot help but change every situation it enters. The truth is like a scalpel that cuts through everything it touches. Love is that same scalpel in the hands of a skilled surgeon. When we handle the truth correctly, we can remove cancerous tumors and mend broken things; but when we handle the truth without caring, we can damage people's lives. What good is it to cut out the cancer if we kill the patient in the process? We should never sacrifice truth just because it is hard or painful, but because sometimes it is hard and painful, we should use great care.

When we present the truth, we should always do it in love, with a heart of compassion and understanding for the lost. When the truth is on your side, and you share it in love and with compassion, you don't have to be defensive about what you are saying, or the way people will react to it. Jesus is truth and He himself came in love. The gospel of Christ is the truth of the ages, and God's greatest act of love towards us.

> *God is not human, that he should lie, not a human being, that he should change his mind. Does he speak and then not act? Does he promise and not fulfill?*
>
> —Numbers 23:19

All or Nothing

Everything about God is truth. Everything in His Word is true, and anything He sets out to do gets completed. Many people want to pick and choose the parts of the Bible, and the parts of being a child of God that they want—the parts they can live with. People want to believe in salvation, but they don't want to believe in hell. They want to believe in an all-powerful God, but they don't believe they have to submit to Him. People want the benefits of Christ, but don't want Christ Himself. To accept Christ, you have to take all of it. If some of the things Christ said in the Bible were wrong, then how can we trust any of the them? Objective truth doesn't leave room for middle ground. Either Christ was the awaited Messiah, or He was a madman.

People like to say they don't believe everything the Bible says about Jesus. They try to discredit the miracles He performed, but say they respect His teachings. Or they say that He was a good man. Let's get something straight—there is no middle ground. Either Jesus is who He says He is, or He is a liar. Or at the very least He is insane. If He is insane He is not the Messiah, and if He lied about one thing we cannot trust any of His teachings. When it comes to truth, it's all or nothing.

Truth Is Always Relevant

The definition of the word *relevant* is:

1. Closely connected or appropriate to what is being done or considered
2. Appropriate to the current time, period, or circumstance; of contemporary interest.

The value of what the gospel communicates transcends time. The gospel is the most important message in the most important book ever assembled. There is a reason why the Bible has never faded away. Its truth is for all generations, and for all times. To minimize the value, importance, and relevance of the gospel message, we have to minimize our need for it. By minimizing and marginalizing the gospel we are saying that either we don't have sin, or that our sinful lives don't separate us from God. Maybe we are saying that we have evolved beyond the needs of our fathers and their fathers before them. Once men feared the plague and they were powerless to stop it, but now through science and our ingenuity, we don't have to worry anymore because we have an antidote. Is this the attitude we have as Christians toward sin?

> *All have sinned and fall short of the glory of God.*
> —Romans 3:23

Whatever breakthroughs are made by science, and no matter what innovations are made in technology, and no matter how intelligent we think we are, we will never lose the need for the true gospel. We won't evolve past it and we won't outgrow it. All men who are born are born into sin, and the only solution for sin is the truth about Jesus Christ. We are so modern though, it is hard for us to humble ourselves to the same solution of our forefathers. Just like with everything else, we want a newer and easier solution. But there is no other solution except for the gospel gift given to us on Calvary.

The Gospel Is Always Relevant

Because it is a timeless truth that Jesus is the only path to salvation and eternal life, it is relevant. It is needed in its purest and truest form in all times. It doesn't need to be dressed up or watered down. It is the only light in the darkness; the only life preserver in a raging sea. The Word of God by the power of the Holy Spirit is full of power and life. Light is always bright in the dark no matter how hip, new, and modern we think that darkness might be. There is power in the gospel of truth unless we distort it, minimize it and marginalize it for the sake of blending in. Light was never meant to fit into the darkness. Actually, light cannot blend in; it was always meant to stand out. We were always meant to stand out.

> *In him was life, and life was the light of all mankind. The light shines in the darkness, and the darkness has not overcome it.*
>
> —John 1:4, 5

I am sure I have in the past, and will in the future, make many mistakes as a preacher. I may say things incorrectly, misunderstand concepts, or accidently take things out of context. I am a mere human with flaws and shortcomings, but one day when I stand before the Savior giving account of my life and ministry, let it never be said that I was afraid to preach the true gospel. Jesus is the only way to God. His birth, death and resurrection paid the price for my sinful life and restored me to the Father. As long as I have air in my lungs, I will preach the truth. I will preach the gospel of Christ Jesus.

CHAPTER 3

THE GOSPEL OF LOVE

Truth without love is brutality, and love without truth is hypocrisy.

—Warren Wiersbe

God proved His love on the cross, when Christ hung, and bled, and died it was God saying to the world "I love you."

—Billy Graham

For God so loved the world that he gave his one and only Son, that whosoever believes in him shall not perish but have eternal life. For God did not send his Son into the world to condemn the world, but to save the world through him.

—John 3:16, 17

There is no possible way to overstate the sheer magnitude of God's love for us. It is hard to even begin to grasp what it meant for God the Father to send His Son Jesus to die for us. There is no event in history as beautiful and passionate as the cross. Forever transforming the cross from the ultimate symbol of loss and shame, into the most enduring image and reminder of Christ's love for us.

We should never take for granted the extreme measures God took to have a relationship with us, to call us His sons and daughters. One of the reasons I believe it is so difficult for us to truly and deeply understand God's love for us, is because it is so contrary to our human nature. Loving someone whose very nature is resistant to yours is hard to grasp. This concept of unconditional love is hard for us to grasp. This is why in Scripture God uses analogies we can understand, like a parent's love for their children, and a husband's burning passion for his wife. These are examples of relationships our human minds can comprehend, but God's love is so much deeper than even these.

We define love in a much different way than God does. Dictionary.com defines love as, *an intense feeling of deep affection; a deep romantic or sexual attachment to someone.* When we have intense feelings towards people, or are attracted to them, we call this love. We say we love people when we are attracted to them, or when they make us feel good. But what happens when that feeling goes away? Or when the person you feel that way towards hurts you or lets you down? This is a mercurial, or an emotional love. Feelings are not a bad thing, but emotions change and if your love is based on them, it will change as well.

Most people's love is conditional. Love is conditional when we require someone to fulfill a condition, or requirement, for us to continue to love them. We tell people we love them because they are beautiful, or because they love us or because they treat us well, because they take care of us, or benefit us in some way. These are all conditions, and if we fail to fulfill these conditions, then our love might fail as well. This kind of love is not based in truth, or in the Lord. This is why people are continually getting divorced. The vow of, "till death do us part" does not mean that at all. What most people really mean is, "Until my feelings change," or "Until you fail to meet my conditions."

People loosely use the term "we fell out of love," but it is impossible to fall out of a commitment. It is a choice you make to go back on your word. Unlike God's love, this brand of love is without fidelity or truth.

God's love is unique. It is completely different than any love you have ever experienced—to try to understand it can be difficult. God's love for you is not based on your performance. You cannot do anything to increase His love for you. God already gave it all, and we could never make Him love us more than He already does. But also, we cannot do anything to make Him love us any less. His love is not based on performance at all.

Jesus gave up His life so that we could be with the Father and experience His love. You can experience the fullness of God's love as soon as you accept Him to be in charge of your life.

God's love is a truth that the human condition can experience on many different levels, but could never fully grasp or explain. That's because it comes from God's perfection which we cannot comprehend no matter how hard we try. In this life, perfection is unattainable for us. This in and of itself makes God's love and Jesus' sacrifice all the more unbelievable. It displays the goodness of God, and exposes us to a kind of love that cannot be found outside of Christ. This is one reason it is hard for us to accept it, because it seems too good to be real. Even though we doubt it, and though we may take it for granted, God's resolve to love us is unbreakable and unchangeable.

> *Whoever does not love does not know God, because God is love.*
>
> —1 John 4:8

"God is love." This portion of Scripture is thrown around by believers and unbelievers alike; but why are people willing to embrace this attribute of God, but ignore so many others? God is also truth; God is also justice; God is also holy. First off, the world we live in has a fundamental misconception of what love is, and who God is. Love to most people speaks of human emotion and feelings, but these feelings come and go. To reduce God's love to a mere human emotion is simply wrong. Emotion is part of love, but love isn't an emotion. It is something much bigger.

Many people use this feeble definition of love that says you're okay, and I'm okay, and God's okay with your sinful and adulterous lifestyle. Saying God doesn't care about what we do isn't saying that God is loving, it is saying that He is indifferent. God's very presence demands holiness, and sin cannot be where He is. God desired to have a relationship with us so He has done everything in His power including paying the ultimate price so we can be in His presence.

A common question of skeptics and believers alike, is the problem of evil and the problem of sin. Why did God even give Eve the opportunity to sin in the garden? It is fairly simple. God desires to have a loving relationship with us, but without freewill and choice there is no love. The reason love is so powerful and beautiful, is because it is a choice.

God has already done everything He could to show us His love, so the idea that God would *make* us love Him and accept Him is preposterous. God made the way, but we have to believe, accept, and surrender to His offer of a relationship with us. Knowing Him intimately, and being known by Him, is what this means. It's more than just knowing *about* Him. Doing His will and pleasing Him is the evidence of your true belief and love for Him. God wants us to know Him, and trust Him, and love Him. This comes from a personal relationship with Him not just doing busy work or ministry.

God wants our heart, and He wants to be first place in our lives—not just using His name to get what we want. Our culture is full of consumerism and the church is no different. God doesn't work for us. He is not a customer service representative. Just because you know about Him, and are well versed in Christianese, doesn't mean you have a real and significant relationship with Him. It takes much more than simply going through the motions.

> *Not everyone who says to me Lord, Lord will enter the kingdom of heaven, but only the one who does the will of my father in heaven. Many will say to me on that day Lord, Lord, did we not prophesy in your name and in your name drive out demons and in your name perform many miracles? Then I will tell them plainly, I never knew you. Away from me you evildoers!*
>
> —Matthew 7:21-23

On that day, He will say, "I never knew you." Not that you didn't accomplish enough, or do enough; not that you didn't give enough money, or you didn't go on enough mission trips, but simply that He never knew you. To know God, and be known by Him in intimate relationship, is what it is all about. This is the love God wishes to share with us. Ministries and projects and evangelism and missions, these things are all important and necessary, but nothing is more important than your intimate and personal relationship with Jesus. We have to define love, who God is, what He expects from us, and how we should relate to Him from the Scripture, not from what we feel or what our culture tells us.

It is clear that God loves us and that He would do anything for us. The question is, do we love Him back and do our actions show it? We can say that we love God all day long, but what do our actions say? If we are the Bride of Christ as the Scripture says, then we should be submitting to Him, honoring Him, praising Him like any loving bride would. Christ has already done His part. He laid down His life for us, He has pursued us, He has made a way for us, and prepared a place for us. Now we could never do enough to deserve His love, or earn what He did for us; but we should be grateful and live a life of submission to Him. Are we pursuing a real and meaningful relationship with Christ or are we merely using Him to get what we want?

> *Submit to one another out of reverence for Christ. Wives, submit yourselves to your own husbands as you do to the Lord. For husband is the head of the wife as Christ is the head of the church, his body, of which he is the Savior. Now as the church submits to Christ, so also wives should submit to their husbands in everything. Husbands, love your wives, just as Christ loved the church and gave himself up for her to make her holy, cleansing her by the washing with water through the word, and to present her to himself as a radiant church, without stain or wrinkle or any other blemish, but holy and blameless. In the same way husbands ought to love their wives as their own bodies. He who loves his wife loves himself.*
>
> —Ephesians 5:21-29

One of the reasons wives sometimes have a hard time submitting to their husbands, is because men are humans and all humans have flaws. Husbands make mistakes, can be selfish, gets things wrong, fall short; he is imperfect. It is only through obedience to Christ that a woman can submit to an imperfect husband by faith. The truth is the more a man lays down his life for his wife, like Ephesians 5 commands, the easier it is for his wife to submit to him.

Why do we have such a hard time submitting to Christ? He is perfect in all of His ways. Never self-serving, He knows all things. He knows everything about you and what is best for you. He laid down His life for you. If we love the Lord with all of our heart, why don't we submit to Him and obey Him? The question is, do we really love Jesus? I mean love Him through personal and intimate relationship? Or do we love what He has done for us, and the benefits being associated with Him provides for us?

Real love is passionate. If you truly and passionately love someone, you will do whatever it takes to please them, to honor them, to make them happy. Especially when everything they have ever done for you has been good for you. Do you love the Lord or do you merely like His benefits? Heaven will be filled with people who love the Lord, who love to worship the Lord. If you don't enjoy praising, and worshiping, and loving the Lord, I have bad news for you. That is what heaven is going to be like.

A question we need to ask ourselves is this, "Would you still want to go to heaven if Jesus wasn't there?" If everything else was there, such as streets of gold, no pain, no tears, no night, and so on. If it was paradise, but without the Savior. If you say yes you would, then maybe you need to examine your heart. Without Jesus being there it wouldn't be paradise. Where He is there is perfect peace; where He is there is love; where He is there is truth.

I'm convinced that many people who claim to be in Christ, but still live in so much discontent, do not really know Him deeply and personally. They are looking for what Christ has to offer, but not Christ Himself. We need to get to know the Lord deeply through His Word, but also through prayer. There is nothing more intimate than prayer. Not repetitious, thoughtless prayer, but through real and intimate conversations with the Savior and lover of your soul. The Father-God who has called you His friend. Show me a man who is struggling to the point of giving up, and I will show you a man whose prayer life needs to grow. This is where, through the spirit, we grow in relationship with the Lord. Prayer is the most intimate way in which we get to know the Lord. Personal prayer time is where love for God is cultivated.

> *Love the Lord your God with all your heart and with all your soul and with all your mind and with all your strength. The second is this: Love your neighbor as yourself There is no commandment greater than these.*
>
> —Mark 12:30, 31

God's love for us is a choice He made a long time ago. He chose to love us, and nothing we ever do will undo His love for us. Not just because He sacrificed so much for us, but because His vow is unbreakable, and He always keeps His word.

On the surface, to an emotional human being, this love seems more like an obligation, and not as strong as an emotional type of love, but ask a parent who chooses to love their child when they act in ways undeserving of love. Their obligation as a parent causes them to love their child even when the child doesn't deserve it. This kind of love is unchanging despite what the other person does or doesn't do.

> *But God demonstrates his own love for us in this: While we were still sinners Christ died for us.*
>
> —Romans 5:8

God didn't place any conditions on us for Him to love us. In fact, true love lays it all out there in spite of whether or not it is received by the other party. This is what makes God's love so unique. That is why in Mark 12:30, 31, we see that what God hopes for, is that we love Him in the same way He loved us—with heart, soul, mind and strength, and to also love others in the same way.

God doesn't ask us to do anything to receive the benefit of His love. He gave it all freely in the hope we would respond to it. He doesn't wait to see what we will do, He loves us unconditionally.

God loved us while we were still sinners, without us having to do anything, simply because He is love. God's nature is love, His character is love. It is so hard for us as humans to understand, but this is the love of the gospel. This is the passion of Christ. This is the will of the Father, that no one should perish, but that all have eternal life with Him. What good is eternal life in the presence of someone you do not love? This is what is misunderstood about the gift of the gospel of love. The gift that is being offered is a place in Father God's family as the bride of Christ. The gift being offered is Christ Himself. Life is the courting process, but you don't get the benefits of being in the family, and sitting at the father's table, if you reject the Bridegroom. Just like the Scripture says:

> *Jesus answered, "I am the way and the truth and the life. No one comes to the Father except through me. If you really know me, you will know my Father as well. From now on, you do know him and have seen him."*
>
> —John 14:6, 7

It seems that many people feel they deserve a place in the family of the Bridegroom they rejected. In fact they want the benefits of Christ but want to remain married to the world. You cannot reject the Bridegroom and still sit at the table with the Father of the Bridegroom. Christ has already forgiven us our infidelity and wants to be in relationship with us. This is why He pursues us. But there will come a day when He will accept our rejection and let us have our own way. Hell is eternal separation from God. God doesn't send anyone there, we choose it ourselves of our own freewill by rejecting His son.

No sin from our past or shortcoming in life can separate us from God's love for us. The only thing that can separate us from the Lord, is us. God wants a real and personal relationship with us, and at the cross He has torn down every barrier that stood in our way. The only thing left is our full surrender and acceptance of His love.

> *For I am convinced that neither death nor life, neither angels nor demons, neither present nor the future, nor any powers, neither height nor depth, neither anything else in all creation, will be able to separate us from the love of God that is in Christ Jesus our Lord.*
>
> —Romans 8:38, 39

CHAPTER 4

THE SIMPLE GOSPEL

> The gospel is so simple that small children can understand it, and it is so profound that studies by the wisest theologians will never exhaust its riches.
>
> —Charles Hodge

> The great question is not 'Will not the heathen be saved if we do not send them the gospel? But, are we saved ourselves if we do not send them the gospel?
>
> —Charles Spurgeon

From the third chapter of Genesis, the plan for Jesus to come as the perfect sacrifice for our sins was set in motion. God's love is a love of action. The Old Testament is full of prophecies, and hopeful yearnings, for the Creator of the world to come back to the earth He created and set things right. The story of Scripture is waiting for the Messiah to come as a sacrifice, documenting His ministry while He was here on earth, documenting His life, death, and resurrection, and waiting for Him to one day return for His church in glory and power.

Even though people still dispute who He was and is, they cannot dispute the fact that Jesus is by far the single best-known person in history. His fame is unparalleled. There is a reason why the Bible is the most sold, the most stolen, most given, and without comparison, the most important book in history. What people say about Jesus, what He taught, what He stood for, and who He really was, varies from person to person. Just like any famous person, speculation and misconceptions about Him are rampant. What people say and what the Bible teaches can be much different.

According to the Bible, Jesus met all the requirements of prophecy and history to be the long-awaited Jewish Messiah. Jesus' life was full of miracles, He was born of a virgin, and out of mercy He healed the sick, raised the dead, and performed many other miracles. He taught with wisdom and authority throughout His three-and-a-half-year ministry. He was betrayed, tortured, and murdered, then He was crucified. After being in a tomb for three days He was raised from the dead and then ascended to heaven, where He sits at the right hand of the Father waiting to someday return and retrieve His church.

The gospel story. There was a time when this doctrine was what other doctrines were built around. It was the rudder and focus of the church; now it seems it is a secondary concept. It is overshadowed by so many less important things, concepts, ideas and, doctrines. While these may be important, they are definitely *less* important than the tenants of our salvation. Without Jesus making the way for our salvation, everything else is pointless and meaningless.

The Gospel

"The time has come," he said. "The kingdom of God has come near. Repent and believe the good news!"

—Mark 1:15

What is the gospel? As I explained in Chapter 2, the word simply means "good news." We refer to this as *the* good news, because it is the best news in history. It is the answer to all of the problems in the world past, present, and future. This, in summary, explains who Jesus is and what He did for us. All hope for the human race is in the gospel of Jesus Christ.

What does it mean to be saved? What does it really mean to be a Christian? Many people today use these terms loosely and incorrectly. To be saved you must first acknowledge that there is something you are being saved from. The gospel preached from many pulpits today doesn't make sense. Many pastors refuse to use words like repentance, sin, and hell. They pervert words like love, grace, and faith. How can you say you are saved if you don't acknowledge you are being saved from destruction—if you don't acknowledge and accept hell as a real place.

We must become aware of our sin and our need for saving. We must repent and turn from our sinful and wicked ways. The Bible says, "Believe in your heart and confess with your mouth that Jesus Christ is Lord." Only then are you a disciple of Jesus. This the gospel; this is Jesus.

The Need Was Great

Our need for saving was great. Every person ever born on planet earth, with the exception of Jesus Himself, was born into sin. We are sinful by nature, so we are separated from a relationship with God. We could never hope to spend eternity with Him, because even one sin disqualifies us from being in His presence. It isn't based on a scale of good and bad works. Many people would say, "I've done a few bad things, but I have done much more good than bad." Unfortunately your good deeds don't make up for your bad, no matter how good or how many there are.

When you do something to hurt someone, apologizing is good,

and doing something to make up for it is nice, but nothing you do will ever truly *undo* what you have done. In the same way, your good deeds don't undo or make up for your bad deeds. We have systems of justice here on earth. God has a justice system as well, but His standard is perfection. Nothing we could ever do could satisfy the need for justice in regard to our sin. It's like being born into billions of dollars of debt, and because of that debt you are put into slavery to pay toward your debt. No matter how hard you work, the interest on your debt is more than you make in a day, or a month, or a year. It's like trying to drain a lake with a cup. No matter how much you drain out it will never be enough; it doesn't even matter.

No one is worthy to go to heaven and be in God's presence. No membership in any church or any religion qualifies us. No one is worthy to be in God's presence. Even calling yourself a Christian and trying to live a good life is not good enough. Only repentance of your sins and accepting Christ as Lord can make you worthy. We are all undeserving of a pardon because of our lives. It's not that God thinks that He is better than us, and above us in every way; it's that God *is* better than us, and above us in every way. God is perfection and His very character demands justice. In God's justice system, the due penalty for sin is death.

> *But now that you have been set free from sin and become slaves of God, the benefit you reap leads to holiness and the result is eternal life. For the wages of sin is death, but the gift of God is eternal life in Christ Jesus our Lord.*
>
> —Romans 6:22, 23

The Character of God

There is no way in this life to completely understand or comprehend the perfection, sovereignty, and holiness of God the Father, the Theos. As we disconnect ourselves from nature, and in our minds believe more and more in our own self-sufficiency, we underestimate God's role and overestimate our own importance in this life. But standing at the foot of the Grand Canyon, or standing at the edge of Niagara Falls we get a sense that maybe we are a small piece of something much greater.

God always has been, and always will be. He created us for His intents and purposes. He is the Creator and we are the created. We really don't have a say in anything. God is holy and perfect and beyond comprehension. Fortunately, He is also good, and His love is without comparison. His holiness is beyond the scope of our understanding, but thankfully so is His love.

People try to rationalize things, they feel entitled to say God's justice and holiness are not fair, and that it violates their human rights, as if the created could say such a thing to the Creator. To allow sin in His presence is impossible, but even if it was possible, how arrogant we would be to ask Him to. But that is exactly what we do.

We are so double-minded and unstable as humans. When we feel our personal rights are violated, we want swift justice and fairness, but when we violate we expect mercy. We should be careful crying out for justice because for us justice means death due to our sin. If we truly understood how desperate our situation was, I believe we would be much more merciful with others. We would share the gospel and work harder to seek and save the lost.

What can we do to be worthy of God's love? Nothing! It is impossible for us but with God all things are possible.

> *When the disciples heard this, they were greatly astonished and asked, "Who then can be saved?" Jesus looked them and said, "With man this is impossible, but with God all things are possible."*
>
> —Matthew 19:25, 26

The Gospel of Jesus Christ

There was not a sacrifice that could satisfy the holiness and justice of God, except God Himself. He gave everything for us, so that we could have relationship with God the Father. His innocence gave Him something we could never have without Him—blamelessness in the sight of God the Father. Through the sinless life He led, His painful death on the cross, and His glorious resurrection, Christ made a the way for us to have the right to boldly approach the Father as a son or daughter.

> *Let us therefore come boldly to the throne of grace, that we may obtain mercy and find grace to help in time of need.*
>
> —Hebrews 4:16

We should boldly, or as the NIV says "with confidence," come to God's throne of grace, because Christ made the way for us to do so. But let's not misunderstand this statement and become arrogant. We should feel secure with the place in God's family that Christ secured for us on the cross, but it should be with a grateful heart, not a prideful or arrogant heart. All things are through Jesus and by the word of Jesus, and through the cross, by which we are saved.

When we ponder the life of Jesus, and all that He has done for us, our hearts should be filled with unending gratitude and thankfulness. Not just for the cross, but for every detail of planning throughout the Old Testament, every moment in history that formed His path to the cross, every sacrifice, every prophecy. You will put your time and effort into the things that truly matter to you. For God, that is *us*. All His time and effort and plans throughout history have been to draw us near to Him. You mattered to God so much, He gave everything to have you. A product is only worth the amount someone is willing to pay for it. You were worth the life of Jesus to God the Father. That is big, because the Father loves the Son so much. God loves you as much as He loves Jesus. The knowledge of this, and this alone, is where we should draw our self-worth from.

Prophecy

Prophecy foretold of the virgin birth of Christ hundreds of years in advance. Jesus was born of a virgin, therefore bypassing the seed of sin. He was *able* to sin, but was not born into sin; although He was able to sin He never did. He was fully human, but still fully God. The Old Testament is full of prophecies about the coming Messiah. Maybe one or two of these Old Testament prophecies could be found in one man, but there are hundreds of them, and Jesus fulfilled all of them. It is amazing that He fulfilled so many prophecies, but what seals the deal about the man of Jesus in prophecy is this. Had there been even one that was not fulfilled, that alone would have been enough to disqualify Him; but over two-thousand years later, it is apparent from Scripture and history that He is the foretold Messiah.

Jesus fulfilled all the Old Testament prophecies about the Messiah.

1. **He would be born of a virgin**
   prophecy-Isaiah 7:14
   fulfillment-Matthew 1:18-25, Luke 1:26-31

2. **He would be born in the town of Bethlehem**
   prophecy-Micah 5:2
   fulfillment-Matthew 2:1, Luke 2:4-6

3. **He would be from the line of Abraham**
   prophecy-Genesis 12:3, Genesis 22:18
   fulfillment -Matthew 1:1, Romans 9:5

4. **He would be a descendant of Isaac**
   Genesis 17:19, Genesis 21:12
   fulfillment-Luke 3:34

5. **He would be a descendant of Jacob**
   prophecy-Numbers 24:17
   fulfillment- Matthew 2:1

6. **He would be from the tribe of Judah**
   prophecy-Genesis 49:10
   fulfillment- Luke 3:33, Hebrews 7:14

7. **He would be heir to King David's throne**
   prophecy-2 Samuel 7:12, 13, Isaiah 9:7
   fulfillment-Luke 1:32, 33

8. **He would flee to Egypt**
   prophecy-Hosea 11:1
   fulfillment-Matthew 2:14, 15

9. **There would be a mass murder of children**
   prophecy-Jeremiah 31:15
   fulfillment- Luke 2:16-18

10. **A messenger would proceed Him**
    prophecy-Isaiah 40:3-5
    fulfillment- Luke 3:3-6

11. **He would be rejected by the Jews**
    prophecy-Psalm 69:8, Isaiah 53:3
    fulfillment-John 1:11, John 7:5

12. **He would be a prophet**
    prophecy-Deuteronomy 18:15
    fulfillment- Acts 3:20-22

13. **He would be called a Nazarene**
    prophecy-Isaiah 11:1
    fulfillment- Matthew 2:23

14. **He would bring light to Galilee**
    prophecy-Isaiah 9:1-2
    fulfillment- Matthew 4:13-16

15. **He would speak in parables**
    prophecy-Psalm 78:2-4, Isaiah 6:9, 10
    fulfillment-Matthew 13:10-15, Matthew 13:34, 35

16. **He would be called King**
    prophecy-Psalm 2:6, Zechariah 9:9
    fulfillment-Matthew 27:37, Mark 11:7-11

17. **He would be betrayed**
    prophecy-Psalm 41:9, Zechariah 11:12, 13
    fulfillment-Luke 22:47, 48, Matthew 26:14-16

18. **The betrayal money would buy a potter's field**
    prophecy- Zechariah 11:12, 13
    fulfillment-Matthew 27:9, 10

19. **He would be falsely accused**
    prophecy-Psalm 35:11
    fulfillment- Mark 14:57, 58

20. **He would be silent before His accusers**
    prophecy-Isaiah 53:7
    fulfillment-Mark 15:4, 5

21. **He would be spit on and struck**
    prophecy-Isaiah 50:6
    fulfillment-Matthew 26:67

22. **He would be crucified with criminals**
    prophecy-Isaiah 53:12
    fulfillment-Matthew 27:38, Mark 15:27, 28

23. **He would be given vinegar to drink**
    prophecy-Psalm 69:21
    fulfillment-Matthew 27:34, John 19:28-30

24. **His hands and feet would be pierced**
    prophecy-Psalm 22:16, Zechariah 12:10
    fulfillment-John 20:25-27

25. He would be mocked by those who crucified Him
prophecy-Psalm 22:7-8
fulfillment- Luke 23:35

26. The soldiers would gamble for his garment
prophecy-Psalm 22:18
fulfillment-Luke 23:34, Matthew 27:35, 36

27. His bones would not be broken
prophecy-Exodus 12:46, Psalm 34:20
fulfillment-John 19:33-36

28. He would be forsaken by God
prophecy-Psalm 22:1
fulfillment-Matthew 27:46

29. He would pray for His enemies
prophecy- Psalm 109:4
fulfillment-Luke 23:34

30. They would pierce His side
prophecy-Zechariah 12:10
fulfillment-John 19:34

31. He would be buried like a rich man
prophecy-Isaiah 53:9
fulfillment-Matthew:27:57-60

32. He would resurrect from the dead
prophecy-Psalm 26:10, Psalm 49:15
fulfillment- Matthew 28:2-7, Acts 2:22-32

33. He would ascend to heaven
prophecy-Psalm 24:7-10
fulfillment-Mark 16:19, Luke 24:51

34. He would be seated at God's right hand
prophecy-Psalm 68:18, Psalm 110:1
fulfillment-Mark 16:19, Matthew 22:44

35. He would be a sacrifice for the sin of everyone
prophecy-Isaiah 53:5-12
fulfillment-Romans 5:6-8

The Incarnation

What a wonderful yet completely mysterious miracle the incarnation of Christ is. The bloodline of all men can be traced back to Adam, and because of his sin, the first man tainted the entire human race with the disease of sin. This is one of the reasons Jesus had to bypass the seed of man.

Jesus, the second person in the holy trinity—the first being God the Father, and the third being the Holy Spirit—took on the form of a man to live among us. Although Christ Jesus took on human form, He has always been and always will be. He predates time. In fact, time is His creation. Jesus was born from the womb of a virgin woman named Mary, although He always was, always has been, and will always be. The incarnation says that the person of Christ Jesus is fully God and fully human and that His two natures are joined together.

> *Therefore the Lord himself will give you a sign: The virgin will conceive and give birth to a son, and will call him Immanuel.*
>
> —Isaiah 7:14

Jesus stepped down from heaven and became flesh. There is no way to overemphasize the sheer magnitude of what this means to us. We have heard this so much, that it almost loses its impact, and we begin to take it for granted. Jesus the Son of God, in obedience to His Father, left behind heaven to come to earth as a baby and grow up into a man. We have to think about how humbling it would be to lay aside His cosmic throne and become a baby. He felt pain and hunger and frustration and all the emotions and trials any human being would. He did so without ever sinning or falling short.

> *In your relationships with one another, have the same mindset as Christ Jesus: Who, being in very nature God, did not consider equality with God something to be used to his own advantage; rather he made himself nothing by taking the very nature of a servant, being made in human likeness. And being found in appearance as a man, he humbled himself by becoming obedient to death, even death on a cross!*
>
> —Philippians 2:5-8

When thinking about the gospel we should never minimize the sacrifice it took to live out a human life from birth to the cross. His death and resurrection are very important, because without the cross and His resurrection we would still be subject to the penalty of our sins. His sacrifice began once He condescended and walked among us. However, the gospel is more than just the cross. It is the life He lived as our perfect example, the compassion He poured out, the prophecies He fulfilled, our sin-debt paid with His crucifixion, and our redemption sealed by His resurrection. He gave it all for us.

A Sinless Life

> *Therefore, since we have a great high priest who has ascended into heaven, Jesus the Son of God, let us hold firmly to the faith we profess. For we do not have a high priest who is unable to empathize with our weaknesses, but we have one who has been tempted in every way, just as we are, yet he did not sin.*
>
> —Hebrews 4:14, 15

One of the earliest creeds of the Christian church is "the Apostles Creed," and although I have nothing against it, in my opinion, it skips over something very important. The creed says, "Jesus was born of the virgin Mary, suffered under Pontius Pilate, was crucified, was dead and buried and was resurrected." These things are true, but he also lived 33 years and ministered for 3 ½ years on the earth and this is just as important as His death and resurrection. The life Christ Jesus lived among us without sinning is one of the parts of His humanity. His sinless life is the pattern for us to compare our lives to.

Jesus lived His life as the perfect example for us to follow. Everything He did on earth shows us how to live in humility, it shows us how to be successful in life and overcome temptation. Jesus didn't do anything we can't do to overcome temptation. When Satan tempted Jesus, He simply quoted Scripture. In fact, He quoted from Deuteronomy. Jesus made it clear that Scripture is the Word of God and contains everything that we need for life and godliness.

> *After fasting forty days and forty nights, he was hungry. The tempter came to him and said, "If you are the Son of God, tell these stones to become bread." Jesus answered,*

> *"It is written: 'Man shall not live on bread alone, but on every word that comes from the mouth of God.'"*
>
> —Matthew 4:3, 4

Jesus overcame temptation, not because He was Jesus, but by the power of the Word of God. Jesus quoted from Deuteronomy 8:3. He demonstrated that there is power in God's Word.

Jesus' sinless life accomplished several things. First of all, for Jesus to be a worthy sacrifice, He had to live a sinless life. Jesus was exposed to all the same situations that any human encountered. He had every opportunity to sin that any of us have. When we minimize this, we minimize His sacrifice. Jesus was hungry, He felt pain, He felt loss, He went through every good and bad thing that every other human does. He never lied, and never sinned throughout thirty-three years of life. Accomplishing this in a fallen world is an amazing feat, but He did it for us. Peter makes it clear that Jesus fulfilled the prophecy spoken about Him in Isaiah 53:9, that He would be blameless and sinless.

> *He committed no sin and no deceit was found in His mouth.*
>
> —1 Peter 2:22

Without His blameless words we wouldn't have His perfect example, and without His sinless life He wouldn't have been qualified to pay our debt of sin on the cross. Jesus did only what the Father told Him to do. Jesus' sinless life was a life of obedience to the Father.

A Life of Miracles

> *Jesus did many other things as well. If every one of them was written down, I suppose that even the whole world would not have room for the books that would be written.*
>
> —*John 21:25*

Jesus did many miracles—too many to count—but the new testament records thirty-five or so specific miracles that Jesus performed throughout the four gospel accounts of His life. Jesus lived for thirty-three and a half years, but His earthly ministry, the time period in which He performed all His miracles, spanned only three and a half years.

Jesus did good wherever He went, not because He was trying to prove anything about who He was or His Lordship. In fact, when people tried to pressure Him to do miracles to prove Himself He not only refused them, He rebuked them. Jesus did fulfill prophecy by healing the sick and performing miracles, but He helped people because He loved people. When Jesus saw people suffering or hurting, He had compassion on them. Jesus helped the hurting because He cared about them. His love was walked out among us. Jesus was doing what came naturally, because His nature is goodness and love.

Everything Jesus has ever done toward us was out of love. Jesus still heals, and still does miracles, because He still cares for us. His love for us is never-fading, unchanged and unending.

The Passion, Death and Resurrection of Christ

Much has been written about the passion of Christ. Scholars and men of greater intellect than I, have said much about this subject.

I will simply give my perspective from Scripture. Everything else in history was just a brick in the path leading to this moment. The passion of Christ was the culmination of a plan set in motion thousands of years before. We must take into consideration the thought, effort, and care the Trinity put into the plan of redemption. It required unyielding dedication and unparalleled passion. Jesus gave everything for us, this truth cannot be overstated. The Creator of the universe traded His life for our freedom. This was the most important act of love in history.

> *He withdrew about a stone's throw beyond them, knelt down and prayed, Father, if you are willing, take this cup from me; yet not my will, but yours be done." An angel from heaven appeared to him and strengthened him. And being in anguish, he prayed more earnestly, and his sweat was like drops of blood falling to the ground.*
>
> —Luke 22:41-44

Jesus endured many things before and during His crucifixion—the pain of betrayal from His disciple and friend Judas, all His other disciples abandoning Him, Peter's denial, being tortured and murdered, bearing the full weight of all the world's sin. But the hardest and most painful part of His entire ordeal was separation from his Father. That moment when God turned His back on Him. This is what I believe Jesus was referring to while praying in the garden, when asked that *this cup* pass from Him. He knew what was coming, and it weighed heavy on Him. Jesus had spent eternity fully connected to His Father. When He came to earth as a human He had a measure of separation from God the Father, but when the sin of all mankind was poured out on Him, God the Father had to turn away from Him for the first time ever. He bore the entirety of all our sin, and all our shame, all at once, and all alone.

Jesus was arrested, beaten, and tortured. He was mocked and spit upon. He was accused of things of which he was innocent, and yet never spoke a word in His own defense. Because He was resolved to obey the Father and determined to save us, He shows meekness and restraint. Jesus is the ultimate example of meekness. Although all power was in His hand, He never used it.

> *Then Pilate took Jesus and had him flogged. The soldiers twisted together a crown of thorns and put it on his head. They clothed him in a purple robe and went up to him again and again, saying, "Hail, king of the Jews!" And they slapped him in the face.*
>
> —John 19:1-3

Jesus was flogged, beaten, mocked, and eventually put to death. He could have stopped it at any time, but because of His passionate love for us, He endured. He endured with our rebellious hearts throughout the Old Testament, He endured as child, and then a man living the life of a human. He endured as everyone abandoned Him and left Him to face His accusers alone. He endured as He was mocked, tortured, and put to death. He endured everything for us. Why then, is it so difficult for us to even endure a slight inconvenience, or endure mild discomfort, for His name sake. A drop of His love outweighs all of ours combined. He endured and still He endures for you and me.

> *For the Lord is good and his love endures forever; His faithfulness continues through all generations.*
>
> —Psalm 100:5

Grace truly is the heart of the gospel, and of the Christian religion, and there is no greater example of this than the cross. It was grace that set His plan to save us in motion in the first place. Grace caused Him to take on flesh and live as a man, but no greater place is grace seen than on the cross.

Jesus died for us while we were His enemies. We were ungodly, unlovable, and selfish, yet Christ willingly died for us. He forgave those who tortured and killed Him, even while dying on the cross. He had mercy on a repentant sinner who cried out while hanging next to Him on the cross. This is Jesus in His glory. God's greatest glory on earth was to suffer, die, and rise again. It is impossible to talk about the gospel and not talk about suffering.

> *You see, at just the right time, when we were still powerless, Christ died for the ungodly. Very rarely will anyone die for a righteous person, though for a good person someone might possibly dare to die. But God demonstrates his own love for us in this: While we were still sinners, Christ died for us.*
>
> —Romans 5:6-8

God knew the perfect time for Jesus to come, according to His plan. What all He set out to accomplish, He did accomplish. Christ died for us and made a way for us to know God in a real and personal way. Relationship has always been God's desire for us.

Jesus' death was precise and purposeful. His plan and intent were clear from the beginning. Jesus died in place of you, and in place of me, not as part of an agreement with us because we loved Him. Jesus died in place of us before we even considered Him, before we even began to identify our need for Him. This is grace, this is love, this is Jesus. In light of this we can conclude that the cross wasn't an act of love among many acts of love. It was *the ultimate act of love* by which all others would be defined. The cross defines love. Jesus laid His life down for us to restore us to the Father. When we become aware of this in our heart, and accept Jesus and His love, we lay down our lives for Him.

It's through the cross that we are ultimately restored to the Father. We receive all the benefits of the gospel through Christ's sacrifice— justification, propitiation, and redemption. This is what Christ accomplished on the cross. Of course, there are many other benefits that trickle down into other areas in our lives, but we should never take these offshoot benefits as being the central reasons. We are able, through Christ, to stand blameless before God. This is the greatest benefit of the gospel, to be counted as righteous to God.

> *Once you were alienated from God and were enemies in your minds because of your evil behavior. But now he has reconciled you by Christ's physical body through death to present you holy in his sight, without blemish and free from accusation.*
>
> *—Colossians 1:21, 22*

The cross is important because of the sacrifice of Christ for us, and because it made us right with God; but equally, if not more important, is the fact that on the third day, Jesus rose from the dead. It isn't just an afterthought of the crucifixion. Without the resurrection, the cross was pointless and powerless. The apostle Paul said this about the resurrection.

> *And if Christ has not been raised, our preaching is useless and so is your faith. More than that, we are then found to be false witnesses about God, for we*

have testified about God that he raised Christ from the dead. But he did not raise him if in fact the dead are not raised. For if the dead are not raised, then Christ has not been raised either. And if Christ has not been raised your faith is futile; you are still in your sins. Then those also who have fallen asleep in Christ are lost. If only for this life we have hope in Christ, we are of all people most to be pitied. But Christ has indeed been raised from the dead, the firstfruits of those who have fallen asleep.

—1 Corinthians 15:14-20

The resurrection is the crescendo of the cross. Christ dying is important, but the resurrection validates everything He said and everything He did. Most especially, His claim to be God. Anyone can die for a cause, but only God could raise Himself from the dead.

Jesus was literally raised from the dead. His body bears witness to this truth. He didn't leave His body, He reclaimed it upon resurrection. When Jesus ascended to heaven, He did so in His body. Before He bodily left this earth, He ate food, and He walked and talked with people. God intended us to be in our bodies, not bodiless souls floating around like cosmic energy. Jesus bears witness to this fact.

The resurrection of Christ bears witness to the workings of the Trinity. Although many elements of the Trinitarian God are mysterious and indefinable, it is obvious that each member of the Trinity played a part in the resurrection of Jesus.

And if the Spirit of Him who raised Jesus from the dead is living in you, he who raised Christ from the

> *dead will also give life to your mortal bodies because of His Spirit who lives in you.*
>
> —Romans 8:11

God the Father is the One who raised Christ from the dead, Jesus was the one who was raised from the dead, and the Holy Spirit is power by which He was raised. This pattern of God doing, by Jesus, through the Spirit, is a pattern that is repeated in other areas of Scripture. In fact, Romans 8:11 tells us that it will be the same way we are raised spiritually and physically. God the Father, in the name of Jesus, will raise us with the power of the Holy Spirit. The resurrection of Jesus is the first fruits of what is to come. It is the pattern for us and our promised resurrection if we are in Christ.

Although we will physically and permanently be resurrected one day, we have already been resurrected spiritually. We are Christ's inheritance, we are already raised from the dead if we are Christians.

> *Since, then, you have been raised with Christ, set your hearts on things above, where Christ is, seated at the right hand of God.*
>
> —Colossians 3:1

While it is true we are waiting for the completion of our faith, the evidence of what is to come is displayed in Christ. Once we lay down our lives, and are reborn into Christ, our future is set in motion and we are raised in Christ. Just like everything in God's economy there is seed, time and harvest. This life is our sanctification, but we are already counted as perfect in His sight due to the death and resurrection of Christ. We are already raised to life with Him and awaiting the harvest.

The Gospel of Christ is the central tenant of our faith. To see any other part of the Christian faith through a proper perspective, we must have this knowing deep in our heart. If we arrive at following Christ from any other perspective, we are in danger of polluting and perverting everything else. Jesus is our mediator and payment for our judgement. The life and person of Jesus, His place in the Trinity, His humanity, His divinity, His death and resurrection, and ultimately the fact that He will return to claim His church, is the cornerstone on which everything else is built. It is the ultimate truth that holds our faith in place.

> *This is good, and pleases God our Savior, who wants all people to be saved and to come to the knowledge of the truth. For there is one God and mediator between God and mankind, the man Christ Jesus, who gave himself as a ransom for all people. This has now been witnessed to at the proper time.*
>
> —1 Timothy 2:3-6

CHAPTER 5

THE CHURCH

The chief danger of the church today is that it is trying to get on the same side as the world, instead of turning the world upside down. Our Master expects us to accomplish results, even if they bring opposition and conflict. Anything is better than compromise, apathy and paralysis.

—A.B. Simpson

He is before all things, and in him all things hold together. And He is the head of the body, the church; He is the beginning and the firstborn from among the dead, so that in everything He might have the supremacy. For God was pleased to have all His fullness dwell in Him, and through Him to reconcile to Himself all things, whether things on earth or things in heaven, by making peace through his blood, shed on the cross.

—Colossians 1:17-20

The face of what the church is has changed quite a bit over the last two-thousand years. From very humble beginnings, full of persecution and uncertainty, to world domination at its height, the church has definitely seen many different shapes and forms. What *is* the church? What is its primary function? What does the Bible say about it? What did Jesus have in mind when He established the church?

The church, in its purest form, is the body of Christ. He is the head of the church. What is the purpose of the church?

- To seek and save the lost, preaching the true gospel to the very ends of the earth
- To disciple God's people through sound teaching of God's Word (the Scripture), though the power of His Holy Spirit
- To correct, rebuke, and encourage believers using God's Word.
- To equip believers to reflect the image of Christ and do good works in the earth
- To be a community of fellowship and safety for God's people to live, serve, and follow Christ together

As a prisoner for the Lord, then, I urge you to live a life worthy of the calling you have received. Be completely humble and gentle; be patient, bearing with one another in love. Make every effort to keep the unity of the Spirit through the bond of peace. There is one body and one Spirit, just as you were called to one hope when you were called; one Lord, one faith, one baptism; one God and Father of all, who is over all and through all and in all.

—Ephesians 4:1-6

Many people across the face of the world, conduct church many different ways. The Bible does lay out some guidelines for what is pleasing and what is orderly for acceptable worship; but many of the things we do in church are based more in tradition than in Scripture. I'm not rebuking traditions or styles of worship, just as long as they line up with God's Word. We should never confuse style with content. Traditions are fine as long as we acknowledge what they are, and never put them on the same level as the Scripture. In my opinion, this is another place that has become more man-centered than God-centered. We should never edit content for the sake of style or tradition, and our content should be based in sound doctrine as found in the Scriptures. So what should church be like?

Tradition, Style, Modes and Methods

Many people get caught up in arguments within the body of Christ. Sometimes these are necessary and important debates. Other times they are over things that are silly and meaningless. These disagreements have sometimes caused rifts or dissensions, and have even caused Christians to be bitter, so much so that Christians completely break fellowship with one another. Some wind up in a painful church split.

What is one of the main reasons for this? Pride and a man-centered view of what the church is for. It fosters a climate and attitude that causes people to be more concerned with how things affect them, rather than how things affect the body, or how things affect God. Pleasing the Lord should be what drives our church, not our wants. We so often confuse tradition with what God really wants, desires, and expects from us. One thing is for sure, Christ established the church and we should not forsake it or His plan and intention.

> *And let us consider how we may spur one another on toward love and good deeds, not giving up meeting together, as some are in the habit of doing, but encourage one another and all the more as you see the day approaching.*
>
> —Hebrews 10:24, 25

Why do we do church the way we do? Some segments within the church do things one way, while others do it a different way. Some services are very long, some are very short. Some people stand in quiet reverence through their service, and others dance, shout and sing. Some churches have full bands and play contemporary music, some sing hymns with organ accompaniment, while others have no music at all. Some have systematic religious observances, while others do not. In some churches the congregation dresses very formally, while others attend church in casual attire. Which way is right and which is wrong? Neither!

The only things that truly matter when it comes to the church is this.

- Does your church preach the real and true Gospel of Jesus Christ?
- Does its theology line up with what God has revealed to you through study of His Word?
- Does your Pastor correlate with the description of what is laid out in 1 Timothy 3:1-7 and in Titus 1:5-9?
- Is your church a community that provides accountability, discipleship, fellowship, encouragement, and love?
- Does your church equip disciples to seek and save the lost?
- Is the main focus worshiping our Lord in spirit and truth

This is truly all that matters. Size doesn't matter, music doesn't matter, only sound doctrine and Christ-centeredness. Everything else is a religious tradition, or a style of worship, and doesn't matter that much.

Why do some churches, on one hand, focus heavily on traditions and liturgy and try to put them on par with Scripture? Why do modern evangelical churches think certain kinds of music or modern and innovative methods mean that their church is more "spiritual" than another? These things are a matter of style or preference, and we have to realize what we should focus on first and foremost—does your church line up with the mandates of Christ in the Bible?

The word *church,* as referred to in the New Testament, comes from a Greek term *ekklesia* which is formed of two Greek words meaning, "an assembly" and "to call out" or "ones who are called out." The church is the body of believers who have been called out of the world by God to live as His children under the authority and power of Jesus Christ, by whose sacrifice we are saved.

> *And God placed all things under his feet and appointed him to be head over everything for the church, which is his body, the fullness of him who fills everything in every way.*
>
> —Ephesians 1:22, 23

If we have been called out as Christ's own, why does it seem that parts of the modern church are trying so hard to fit in with the world, to look like the world, to be accepted by the world? You don't reach the lost in a dark world by dimming your light. Jesus living in you should be the light shining through you. Many say that these are just modes of spreading the gospel, but if we aren't living righteous lives that look like Jesus' life, then we are wasting our time. We should be living out the fruit of the Spirit. Jesus spent time with sinners, but he never sinned. His character didn't change.

> *They are not of the world, even as I am not of it. Sanctify them by the truth; your word is truth. As you have sent me into the world, I have sent them into the world. For them I sanctify myself, that they too may be truly sanctified.*
>
> —John 17:16-19

The church is a body and a community of believers who live by the truth. The Bible doesn't tell us to withhold the truth for the sake of evangelism, or water down the truth to make outsiders feel comfortable when they attend. We should speak the uncut truth from the pulpits of our churches. We must speak the truth in love, but love doesn't mean we edit the truth. That is counterintuitive of what love really is. Love is doing right by others, even when it is not easy. Christ is the truth and if we minimize the truth, water down the truth, or leave parts of the truth out in order to be tolerant of this world's climate, or to conform to this world's pattern, we are degrading what Christ died for. We should be changing the world, not be changed by it. Withholding the truth about the gospel to spare someone's feelings isn't love; it is showing you care more about their reaction than their soul.

> *Do not conform to the pattern of this world, but be transformed by the renewing of your mind. Then you will be able to test and approve what God's will is, his good, pleasing and perfect will.*
>
> —Romans 12:2

God is not pleased when we are worldly and when we conform to what the spirit of the age says is acceptable. The Christ-centered gospel is one of love, passion, sacrifice, suffering, and self-denial. The church should be presenting a gospel that conforms people to Christ, not a false gospel that attempts to conform the character of Christ and His teachings to the world.

Church of the Consumer

The world today is full self-centered people, and although this isn't unique to our time, it seems to have become more blatant than in the years past. It also seems to be infiltrating the church like never before. Many televangelists and preacher-authors, are writing self-centered books that focus on us and our importance, rather than the importance of Christ. In America we live in a capitalistic, consumer-based society. Nothing's wrong with that, except when we adopt that attitude within the walls of the church. Church isn't a product that we consume, it is a community of which we are a part. It's a family to which we all belong. It shouldn't matter what the society's conditions are, what kind of economic system is in place, or what kind of regime is in rulership, the church should preach the same gospel, no matter what.

Many people today shop for churches like they shop for products at a mall. Do they have the amenities I want? Do they preach the kind of messages I want to hear? Do they cater to my wants? Do they have all the programs I desire? And in turn, many churches have gotten the message and have begun formatting the church to please the consumer. This is an abomination. People should seek God about where they should attend church and where they should serve. We should be more concerned about what we are bringing to the house of the Lord than what we get out of it.

The church, on the other hand, should be a beacon of truth and life, preaching the uncompromised message of truth according to the Scriptures as led by the Spirit. It should be a community for fellowship and friendship. It should be a source of help and blessing for the community, always reaching out to the poor and the hurting. But all of that should be built around a message of uncompromised truth. If we edit the content that is preached, just so we don't offend people, or so we can attract more people, than we are not Christ's church.

The church today has been infiltrated by a new gospel, a different gospel than the one by which we were saved. It's a gospel without the need for repentance, a gospel that tolerates a sinful lifestyle. A gospel with a God that wants to empower your will, instead of laying down your will and picking up your cross. A God that is portrayed to be a magical genie who exists to grant your wishes. A God who wants everyone to be rich. It seems we are willing to do anything to fill the seats of our churches. This is not the sovereign God of the Bible. I'm not saying that there is anything wrong with having a large church with lots of programs, and lots of cool stuff going on. I'm saying that if your church compromises the truth in order to please man rather than preaching the truth in order to please God, you are doing more damage than good.

The Church of Entertainment

Let me start off by saying I'm not against entertainment. It is healthy to have personal times of recreation. I have had more fun as a Christian than I ever could have imagined before knowing Christ. Just like everything else in life, all things should be done in moderation. Nowadays though, it seems as though entertainment is not an extra; people expect everything to be entertaining. This goes beyond mere recreation and borders on escapism. We expect to be entertained, catered to, and pacified. We don't have time to wait on the Lord, or pray through until God moves. Doesn't God realize that we are on a schedule and that we have important things to do? We are busy and we are important. If God, or the church we attend, doesn't entertain us and meet our expectations as a customer, we will just take our business elsewhere.

This attitude is troubling to say the least. One of the core reasons for this is an improper perspective of the cross. I'm not saying you can't enjoy church. I love going to the House of the Lord; but I love going to church because it is an opportunity to meet with Lord in community with my brothers and sisters in Christ. To go to the altar and seek God's face and His will with my spiritual family. To hear God's Word preached from the pulpit. To be corrected, rebuked, and encouraged by the Holy Spirit. To pray for my brothers and sisters in the faith. To be prayed for by my brothers and sisters in the faith. To be a disciple, to be a worker, to be a laborer of the gospel.

There was a time when church was worshiping, preaching, praying, and being led by the Spirit. Now some churches are so rehearsed and scheduled, there is no time for a move of the Spirit—it's not in the order of the service. I am all for order and excellence, but we should always purposefully leave room for the Spirit. We are fat, wealthy, and comfortable but inside we are bankrupt wretches.

Instead of pastors fasting, praying, and seeking the Lord about what should be preached to the people, we hire consulting firms to tell us what people enjoy hearing from the pulpit. We take polls that ask questions like, "What kind of songs to do you want to hear?" "Do you want modern music or traditional music?" "What length of service are you comfortable with?" "What topics make you uncomfortable and would prefer not to hear?" "What topics would you like to hear from the pulpit?"

This is absurd! The first work of the Holy Spirit is conviction, which leads to repentance, which leads to salvation. And even those of us who are saved and serving Christ, still need to feel the conviction of the Holy Spirit from time to time to help keep us on track and moving toward the mark. Consulting groups, church growth strategies, and well-rehearsed entertainment take up all the time in our forty-five minute to one-hour services. Who has time to seek the face of the Lord, prostrate ourselves at the altar, or get lost in worship?

Some churches today are so full of entertainment and gimmicks, it's sad and embarrassing. They come up with flashy gimmicks and desperately try to insert a Scripture or two to add validity to their message. It's empty, and mostly powerless. We as a culture are addicted to entertainment, and it's becoming more so in the church. Television, the Internet, video games, cell phones, movies, music—anything to avoid quiet reverence before the Lord. We feel like we have to fill every second of our services with one gimmick after another.

The last thing we need is more entertainment, especially in the church. We should be very careful using secular methods to try and grow a church, because what will result will be something worldly. The church has fallen out of love with the Lord and in love with the world. Excusing our actions with God's grace, we fulfill the lust of the flesh, the lust of our eyes, all the while, with pride and arrogance, we say that all is well. We excommunicated conviction and repentance from the church because they weren't entertaining or encouraging.

> *Do not love the world or anything in the world. If anyone loves the world, the love for the Father is not in them. For everything in the world; the lust of the*

> *flesh, the lust of the eyes, and the pride of life, comes not from the Father but from the world. The world and its desires pass away, but whoever does the will of God lives forever.*
>
> —1 John 2:15-17

The question is this: How much is the church we attend influenced by the world? Is our church entertainment-driven? Are we concerned with holiness anymore? The church once was very legalistic which was wrong. We had a performance-based and works-based theology. Now the pendulum has swung so far the other direction, to the point where anything goes. Let us not confuse legalism with holiness.

As a culture, we love to be entertained. Music and drama can be used as amazing elements to express truth, or lead people towards Christ. Music is one of my favorite elements in worship. I am a musician, and my wife is as well. We got our start in ministry as worship pastors. We love music and worshiping God in song. We have spent hours lost and immersed in worship to the Lord, but that is not what I'm referring to here. Using music as an avenue to worship God in spirit and truth is one thing. I'm referring to the act of outrightly using entertainment to grow churches and fill pews. But true worship is nowhere to be found. And, it seems, neither is Jesus.

Pastors in the pulpit wear clothing that promotes worldly movies, worldly bands, and music that glorifies, drug use, drinking, gang violence, fornication, sexual immorality, foul language, taking the Lord's name in vain and outright blasphemy. And it's all in the name of being relevant.

Cursing, yes, I said cursing from the pulpit. Quoting actors and musicians from the pulpit whose lifestyles and words are contrary to the Lord and even blasphemous and crude. Using crude language to illustrate points. Constantly telling jokes that are out of line.

We refuse to be somewhere that doesn't entertain us and when you mention these sorts of things to some young, hip ministers they get defensive and usually say something like, "You're being legalistic. Don't worry I'm covered by grace. As long as Holy Spirit doesn't convict me it's not wrong for me."

Some of the entertainment that has seeped into the church, is not only vile and in contrast to the character of Christ, but outright mocks our Savior. How could we ever let this happen? They are saying everything is all right— but it's not. If you think that what you look at and listen to does not affect you, then you are blinded to the truth by your own wicked desires.

> *The eye is the lamp of the body. If your eyes are healthy, your whole body will be full of light. But if your eyes are unhealthy, your whole body will be full of darkness. Then if that light within you is darkness, how great is that darkness!*
>
> —Matthew 6:22, 23

Entertainment-driven churches focus on pacifying people. Arrogant attitudes that are full of pride and full of the world, gloss over truths about repentance, suffering with Christ, and sin. They always give an upbeat, relevant, and encouraging message to keep the seats full and the church growing. This is a form of godliness, but it's powerless and worthless. Without the gospel, the church is powerless. This is the church spoken about in 2 Timothy that has a form of godliness, but denies its power.

> *But mark this: There will be terrible times in the last days. People will be lovers of themselves, lovers of money, boastful proud, abusive, disobedient to their*

> *parents, ungrateful, unholy, without love, unforgiving, slanderous, without self-control, brutal, not lovers of the good, treacherous, rash, conceited, lovers of pleasure rather than lovers of God, having a form of godliness, but denying its power. Have nothing to do with such people.*
>
> —2 Timothy 3:1-5

What is the power they deny? It is the gospel. It is Jesus crucified on a cross and raised again on the third day. The cross is the dividing line between a church full of power, anointing, and the Holy Spirit, and a social club full of customers looking to be fed. If the church wants real revival, and a resting anointing of the Holy Spirit who moves in power, we have to refocus on a Christ-centered gospel. We must humble ourselves, become people of prayer, repent, and turn from our wickedness. God will give us real grace if we will humble ourselves. He will put His favor back into our lives and back into the church. The success of a church isn't dictated by the number of people sitting in the seats, but the heart condition, and the character of the people sitting in them.

The church has endured through the ages. Through false doctrines, through persecution, through suffering. The church has the power of the Holy Spirit to sustain it, so there is no doubt whether or not the church will endure. It's only a question of whether or not we are part of Christ's true church. Christ's true church is filled with disciples, and we are His disciples if we obey His commandments. Christ's true church isn't filled with church club members, or consumer Christians, or social Christians. It is filled with people who truly know the Lord, and are known by the Lord. His sons and daughters who fill His house to worship and serve Him.

The church is still God's platform for the gospel in the earth, and in spite of its flaws and shortcomings, it is still the Bride of

Christ. The church is made up of flawed and imperfect people who make mistakes, but as long as Christ is the head of the church, and we teach the Word, and preach the cross, we will be salt and light to a lost and dying world. If we are not the light and salt, we are good for nothing.

> *You are the salt of the earth. But if the salt loses its saltiness, how can it be made salty again? It is no longer good for anything, except to be thrown out and trampled underfoot.*
>
> *You are the light of the world. A town built on a hill cannot be hidden. Neither do people light a lamp and put it under a bowl. Instead they put it on its stand, and it gives light to everyone in the house. In the same way let your light shine before others, that they may see your good deeds and glorify your Father in heaven.*
>
> —Matthew 5:13-16

CHAPTER 6

THE PROSPERITY GOSPEL

> The true gospel is a call to self denial, it is not a call to self fulfillment.
>
> —John Macarthur

> We can stand affliction better than we can prosperity, for in prosperity we forget God.
>
> —D.L. Moody

> No one can serve two masters. Either you will hate the one and love the other, or you will be devoted to the one and despise the other. You cannot serve both God and money.
>
> —Matthew 6:13-16

Over one hundred years ago, Charles Spurgeon said, "I believe that it is anti-christian and unholy for any Christian to live with the object of accumulating wealth." In spite of this train of thought, many preachers, churches, and ministries have an entirely opposite view, even going so far as to say that accumulating wealth is evidence of your right standing with God. This brand of theology comes in many different forms, and some are more blatant than others. But it is a way of thinking that all Christians should be physically healthy, monetarily wealthy, and mentally happy at all the times. The believe-and-receive message, the blab-it and grab-it gospel; the prosperity gospel.

I believe in the prosperity of the Lord on His people. I believe that God is a good Father as He states in Matthew 7:11, but the obsession some have with wealth is unhealthy, and goes beyond the blessing of the Lord. It seems that instead of living by faith in the Provider we pray that He bless us with enough provision so that we won't need Him anymore. We should accumulate as much as possible and build bigger and bigger barns. This doesn't sound much like the words of Jesus. Although I am opposed to this hyper-prosperity message, it doesn't mean I pray for poverty. I pray that God give me what I need and bless me with what I can be faithful with. The Scripture says:

> *And my God will supply all your needs according to the riches of His glory in Christ Jesus.*
>
> —Philippians 4:19

There is a big difference between God supplying all of your needs, and you getting everything you ever wanted. I don't believe in a prosperity gospel, nor do I believe in an overly pious and falsely humble poverty gospel. I believe in God's provision for His people.

One of the key areas the prosperity gospel has confused, is faith. It reduces faith to something so small that we think of it as the magic ingredient needed to get all the things we ever wanted. Faith is so much more than just getting stuff. Faith comes from hearing God's Word, and not just hearing with physical ears, but also with spiritual ears. Faith is taking what is promised in God's Word as true. Faith pleases God because it is your true acceptance of His goodness and love. Faith is putting action behind your thoughts and words in regard to God.

At their worst, preachers of this faulty theology, speak about faith like it is something you can amass, just like the earthly treasures they seek to amass. They believe if you have enough faith, you can demand God to bless you and to move on your behalf. Sound doctrine says faith has more to do with justification before God, than accumulating worldly wealth and possessions here on earth. And as far as commanding or demanding the Lord to do your bidding, nothing is more arrogant and foolish.

> *Do not store up for yourselves treasures on earth, where moths and vermin destroy, and where thieves break in and steal. But store up for yourselves treasures in heaven, where moths and vermin do not destroy and where thieves do not break in and steal. For where your treasure is, there your heart will be also.*
>
> —Matthew 6:19-21

Just like the Scripture says, what you care about in your heart is what you will concern yourself with, your time, your energy and your money. Why sacrifice what is truly important, in order to chase worldly treasure that is here today and gone tomorrow. Rather build up eternal treasures. But maybe we don't, simply because we are not concerned with eternal things.

Praying that you receive a blessing isn't necessarily wrong, but the problem is we have turned prayer into a time where we give God our list of wants like an entitled child who pouts when he doesn't get his way. This idea of thinking faith is the currency that gives us the ability to demand what we want from God is foolish, to put it nicely.

Prosperity preachers try and use God's covenant with Abraham as a basis for this erroneous doctrine. They cite Scriptures like Galatians 3:14 where it says: *"He redeemed us in order that the blessing given to Abraham might come to the Gentiles through Christ Jesus."* But they leave out the second half of the verse which clearly explains what he is talking about: *"so that by faith we might receive the promise of the Spirit."* This is obviously talking about salvation, not monetary gain. This gross misuse of the Scripture happens over and over again. This is because their idea of the gospel is centered around themselves, rather than centered around Christ. It is easy for them to make this leap because they only focus on the parts of Scripture that they can manipulate to fit what they want to hear. Their minds always go to monetary riches instead of spiritual riches, because that is what their hearts desire. The greatest treasure in life is to find our security and value in Christ and Him alone. Money itself means nothing to the Lord, He only talks about it so much because He understands its value to a heart that trusts Him, and its value to a heart that doesn't

Giving to Receive

In my opinion, this is one of the most obvious and blatant places where the prosperity message gets things wrong. What is the purpose of giving? To hear some preachers tell it, we give so we can receive. They imply that the blessing of the Lord is not just a byproduct of giving, but that it is the *reason* for giving.

With riches comes burdens and responsibilities. When we say acquiring wealth is something we should strive for, I would say that is contrary to the teaching of Scripture. We should give because it honors God. We should give because God is giving, and we want to be like Him. The main thing we should realize is that everything we have comes from God and belongs to God.

The tithe (which is ten percent of your income), belongs to God and isn't *giving* at all. God requires it. The other ninety percent is what God has given you to be a steward over. However, stewardship isn't the same as ownership. We will give account one day of how we stewarded what God entrusted to us, whether that be money, time, relationships, or the gospel. We should we very careful in what order we prioritize those things.

It comes down to your perspective. Are we living for this life, or is our hope in our future with Christ? Are we doing what God has put us here on earth to do—spreading the gospel, serving the Lord, and serving others—or are we simply here to build our castle, and our kingdom, and serve ourselves?

This comes back to the original point of this book. The prosperity gospel makes the gospel of Christ about us, about how it benefits us, about how it makes us rich. The true gospel is selfless and giving, and based on unconditional love. Jesus gave without expectation. The most important benefit of the true gospel is the gift of Christ Himself. The fact that He will never leave you or forsake you, and that you will spend eternity with Him. Of course, God cares about us and will supply our needs. In fact, Jesus speaks about our needs in an inconsequential way—not with indifference, but almost like He is saying that supplying our needs is a no-brainer. Of course, God will supply our needs, because He loves us. We shouldn't worry so much about ourselves. God truly is in control and will take care us.

> *Therefore I tell you, do not worry about your life, about what you will eat or drink; or about your body, what you will wear. Is not life more than food, and the body more than clothes? Look at the birds of the air; they do not sow or reap or store away in barns, and yet your heavenly Father feeds them. Are you not much*

> *more valuable than they? Can any of you by worrying add a single hour to your life?*
>
> *And why do you worry about clothes? See how the flowers of the field grow. They do not labor or spin. Yet I tell you not even Solomon in all his splendor was dressed like one of these. If that is how God clothes the grass of the field, which is here today and tomorrow thrown into the fire, will he not much more clothe you, you of little faith? So do not worry saying what shall we eat? Or what shall we drink? Or what shall we wear? For the pagans run after all these things, and your heavenly Father knows that you need them. But seek first His kingdom and His righteousness, and all these things will be given to you as well. Therefore do not worry about tomorrow, for tomorrow will take care of itself. Each day has enough trouble of its own.*
>
> —Matthew 6:25-34

Jesus' words in Matthew 6:25, *"Don't worry about your life,"* is in direct opposition to the prosperity gospel. In Matthew 6:32, Jesus tells us not to run after material possessions like the pagans do. Time and time again, the prosperity message is in stark contrast to that of Jesus Himself.

Prosperity preachers focus solely on comfort, happiness, and wealth in this life; they rarely talk about eternity. They tend to only focus on our living conditions, but speak little about the condition of our soul. They focus on their living situation first, and becoming rich at the expense of their congregation by preaching this message of worldly gain.

I am not against preachers making a living, even making a good living. I am a preacher and want to provide for my family and make a comfortable life for them. But not off the backs of the poor and the disenfranchised, or even by manipulating the rich and greedy. The Scripture does say that riches of the wicked are laid up for the righteous, but I will leave the distribution of wealth to God.

Although the price of the gospel wasn't cheap, it is freely given and not sold. Jesus already paid the price in full. We cannot give our way into favor with God. Right standing with God is only obtained through the cross of Christ. Saying that there is an additional cost is a slap in the face of Christ and the sacrifice He made for us. Jesus paid the price in full. The house of the Lord should be a house of prayer, a house of truth, not a money-making venture.

> *When Jesus entered the temple courts, he began to drive out those who were selling. It is written, He said to them, My house will be a house of prayer; but you have made it into a den of robbers.*
>
> —Luke 19:45, 46

Giving to the church is important. Not because we hope it makes us rich, but because it is the house of the Lord. God loves a cheerful giver, not a manipulated giver. I know that money is necessary in our world, and I have great respect for the many men and women that I know who are business owners and run companies, and who are dedicated Christ followers and church members. They are honest people and good stewards of what God has given them. There is nothing wrong with living in a nice house and driving a nice car as long as it is within your means. But those of us who are ministers need to be very careful that we do not use our position as pastors, evangelists, and preachers as a means to get rich. The gift of the gospel is free to anyone who will repent and follow Jesus Christ. Looking at the life of Jesus and the message of Jesus, how

He preached and how He lived, is a great starting point to show the great contrast of this type of theology and the words of our Lord.

One Thing You Lack

We as a culture are obsessed with monetary success. It is not just money itself that entices people, it's everything that comes with it—respect, influence, and power. Wealth opens doors and creates access for the one who has it. It not only creates visions of physical security, but also seems to bring peace of mind that no calamity will be able to overtake you. Although it seems to be more rampant than ever, it is nothing new.

In Mark 10:17-27, we find the story of a man who seemed to have everything going for him. He finds Jesus on the street and it seems with sincerity and humility, this wealthy young man approaches Jesus to seek wisdom about how to inherit eternal life. He gets off to a rough start with Jesus when he precedes his question by addressing Jesus as, "good teacher." Jesus replies with a question, "Why do you call me good?" Then Jesus says "No one is good--except God alone."

Jesus confronts the man right off the bat. He knew the man didn't understand that he was talking to God. Jesus also wanted to confront the man's notion of good. People in that day, and today, look at people like this young man as being good men; men who mostly do right and have a good heart. These same people view Jesus as the Lord of people who are mostly good. They believe Jesus knows their hearts and understands and approves.

Wealth not only clouds the rich person's view of themselves, but also sometimes our view of them for the better. But not Jesus. Like a physician of the soul, He doesn't give encouraging words that are false like so many might. He immediately identifies the area that will keep this man from eternal life and He confronts him with it.

THE PROSPERITY GOSPEL

At a glance, this guy probably seemed like the perfect candidate to be part of Jesus' ministry. He was humble, he seemed to reverence and honor Jesus. He apparently had money and influence, and probably could have helped finance their travels and the ministry. In today's church, he would have been given a place of prominence and influence. But Jesus puts His finger on the flaw that will stop this man from following Him, and confronts him. Why does Jesus do this? It's because Jesus cared about him.

If a problem is not identified, it can never be corrected. Why do we, as humans, resist correction? It's because deep down no one is good, we are all selfish and corrupt and in need of the Lord. We were born into sin, and to inherit eternal life we must be born again into Christ.

Wealth isn't necessarily evil but it can keep us from seeing how needy we are. Our Lord speaks about being rich like it is a burden, not something we should seek. He goes so far as to say it is very difficult for a rich man to enter the Kingdom of Heaven. In the letter to the Philippians, Paul explains that everything he had before Christ, now seems like garbage to him compared to the surpassing glory of knowing Christ.

When Jesus told the young rich man what he lacked, it says that Jesus loved him. In love, Jesus told this man the truth about his heart. He gave him the same opportunity He had given the others; to lay down their lives, pick up their cross, and follow Him.

The man felt comfortable in his own goodness. He had to be confronted to see his own need, to see his own lack. Heaven isn't filled with people who are *mostly good*. Heaven is filled only with people who surrendered to Jesus, who accepted adoption into the family of God through Christ's death and resurrection.

> *Jesus looked at him and loved him. "One thing you lack" He said. "Go, sell everything you have and give to the poor, and then you will have treasure in heaven. Then come follow me."*
>
> *At this the man's face fell. He went away sad, because he had great wealth.*
>
> —Mark 10:21, 22

Jesus loved him and He loves us too, but when we say we want to follow Him, He confronts us with what we lack. The question is, will we sell our treasure and give it away to follow Him? Or will we go away sad?

Although this man said he wanted to inherit eternal life, his heart wasn't focused on eternity. Jesus didn't say give away all your wealth for nothing. He said sell all you have and give to the poor, and then you will have treasure in heaven. But the man didn't value treasure in heaven as much as he valued wealth, power, and influence that came along with riches here on earth.

In Matthew 6, Jesus says not to store up treasure here on earth because it isn't permanent, but to store up treasure in heaven because it is eternal. Then He says where your treasure is there your heart will be also. Where is your heart? On eternity with Jesus or on some treasure you have put before following the Savior. Jesus uncovers the worldly treasures deep in our heart the way only He can, and in love gives us a choice. To leave it behind and follow Him, or to keep it and go away sad.

A Feel-Good Message

Our society has tons of prescriptions, seminars, books, speakers, programs, systems, and forms of escapism to make us happy. The prosperity message is a feel-good message, because the goal is to fill the seats in the church and make people feel good—to be encouraging no matter what. We shouldn't encourage the lost in their sins. We should not be so concerned about how many people come to our church as much as we should be concerned with discipling the ones God has entrusted to us. Of course, many of these feel-good churches are full of people and are steadily growing. They love to hear what their itching ears want to hear from the pulpit week after week. Growth in numbers isn't a good indicator of a healthy church.

> *For the time will come when people will not put up with sound doctrine. Instead, to suit their own desires, they will gather around them a great number of teachers to say what their itching ears want to hear. They will turn away from the truth and turn aside to myths.*
>
> —2 Timothy 4:3, 4

Jesus was always clear about who He was speaking to. He made distinctions between sheep and goats, wheat and tares, plants and weeds. Jesus preached repentance, judgement and salvation. He made it clear when he said:

> *Whoever is not with me is against me, and whoever does not gather with me scatters.*
>
> —Matthew 12:30

Feel-good preachers, and prosperity preachers, fail to distinguish between the saved and the lost. They speak to everyone the same, because the goal is to encourage and make everyone feel good. If an atheist, or a person whose life is filled with bondage and sin, can come to your church week after week and leave feeling encouraged, then you are not preaching the same gospel Jesus preached. You are preaching a deluded doctrine where happiness outweighs holiness, and serving yourself outweighs serving God.

Positive Confession

The power of positive confession is deeply tied to the prosperity gospel. This is a place where a lot of confusion comes up because of a very careless handling of the Scriptures. If you speak it, it will come to pass. If you believe it you will receive it. Unless, of course, you are lacking in faith. This heretical teaching probably brings more confusion than any other.

I know that some of you are asking this question right now—but what about Proverbs 18:21?

> *The tongue has the power of life and death, and those who love it will eat its fruit.*
>
> —Proverbs 18:21

I'm glad you asked. The Scripture says that the tongue has power and I believe that to be true. Your words breathe life or death into every situation in your life. Your words can bring restoration to someone who has been wounded. An encouraging word can give someone the life they need to endure another day. Words of warning and wisdom can save someone from actions that bring deadly consequences. Words can also damage. Words that are harshly spoken in anger can kill a friendship or a marriage.

I am Charismatic and Pentecostal in my theology. I believe in the power of prayer. I believe that God is the same yesterday, today, and forever. I believe in miracles and that the power of the Holy

Spirit works through people to accomplish God's will in the earth. I believe the power of God is limitless and absolute.

Sometimes it's not a case of the positive-confession preachers preaching false doctrine (although many of them do), but it's more of a case of putting emphasis in the wrong place. Or it's a case of over-emphasizing certain things just to make their point, and to attempt to make Scripture fit their theology.

The Scripture says our words have power, but nowhere does it says that power is absolute, nor does the Scripture say that our words have *creative power*. Only God has creative power. Now we might say that we create things as humans, but that is just an expression. We can make things only out of other things. God alone can create things with His words. To create something is to make something out of nothing. If you think your words can create something out of nothing, go over to an empty lot and speak a house into existence. You will be sorely disappointed. The power of confession message isn't new and has come around in many different packages over the years. It is pagan in origin and is practiced by Wiccan covens, The New Age Movement, and New Thought Philosophy

The hyper-positive confession movement is just a repackaged New Thought philosophy known as "the law of attraction." The law of attraction can be summed up with this phrase "like attracts like." They believe by focusing on positive or negative thoughts, a person brings positive or negative experiences into their lives. This belief and train of thought is based on the idea that people and their thoughts are, at their core, made up of *pure energy,* and like-energy attracts like-energy. Even though positive-confession preachers try to make this train of thought sound biblical it is not. It does not line up with the Bible.

I am all for being positive and optimistic. I do believe the things we say have an emotional, mental, and even spiritual impact on us and the people around us. I also believe in praying for miracles. God is the same yesterday, today and forever. Anything that was possible in the Bible is possible today. With God all things are possible. We can pray for the sick to be healed, we can speak and cast out demons, we can move mountains. But not because we are powerful, but because God is all powerful and living in us.

Understand this though. Our words are powerful, and we will give an account for the things we do, but also the things we say during our time on earth. Jesus put a great emphasis on our words.

> *But I tell you that everyone will have to give account on the day of judgement for every empty (or idle) word they have spoken. For by your words you will be acquitted, and by your words you will be condemned.*
>
> —Matthew 12:37

We will be judged by our words. Also, we can have a great impact with our words. We are saved partly by the confession of our mouth, so the mouth is powerful, but we are not able to make something out of nothing. Only God can literally materialize something. We must be very careful not to misuse our sonship in Christ. Just because God has graciously made a way for us to approach God, we must still do so with respect and honor. When we think our words have the power, or the right, to tell God what to do, we are far away from the truth.

The Value of Contentment

One of the subtle poisons of this the prosperity message is a nonstop unquenchable hunger for more, more, more. They pray for more prosperity, but rarely will one of these preachers teach the value of properly managing what God has already blessed you with, or the value of being content.

> *Then he said to them, Watch out! Be on guard against all kinds of greed; life does not consist in an abundance of possessions.*
>
> —Luke 12:15

> *Keep your lives free from the love of money and be content with what you have, because God said, Never will I leave you; never will I forsake you.*
>
> —Hebrews 13:5

Nowhere in God's Word does it tell us that we should seek riches. Nowhere did Jesus preach that we should strive to be rich. In fact, the Scripture warns over and over again about the pitfalls of money, and the danger of riches. Money itself is not evil, but a lack of contentment about what God has given you is greed, and greed is a sin. The love of money is a false gospel that drives people from true faith.

> *But godliness with contentment is great gain. For we brought nothing into the world and we can take nothing out of it. But if we have food and clothing, we will be content with that. Those who want to get rich fall into temptation and a trap and into many foolish and harmful desires that plunge people into ruin and destruction. For the love of money is a root of all kinds of evil. Some people, eager for money, have wandered from the faith and pierced themselves with many griefs.*
>
> —1 Timothy 6:6-10

Preachers concerned only with the here and now and not eternity, will rarely speak of contentment, because they are much more concerned about a person's current condition than the condition of their eternal soul. Everything is about the here and now. It is self-centered, not God-centered—concerned with getting everything you want in the here and now. Today it seems success is determined by your position in life and your possessions, not the content of your character, or your right standing with God. This is why Jesus preached about sin so much, because eternity was His focus. This is why, in meekness, He came and gave His life for us.

> *Jesus answered them, It is not the healthy who need a doctor, but the sick. I have not come to call the righteous, but sinners to repentance.*
>
> —Luke 5:31, 32

Jesus constantly called out to sinners to repent, because He wasn't here to raise up an earthly kingdom. He was here to seek and save the lost, and that is what we should be doing as well. Preaching the truth. Preaching tough messages. Preaching hard messages.

> *I tell you, no! But unless you repent, you too will all perish.*
>
> —Luke 13:3

The message of repentance isn't very popular today. Jesus cared about people enough to be honest, to tell them the truth no matter what, because He loved them. Do we? Do we love the lost enough to tell them the truth, even when they call us fools? Prosperity is not real prosperity if you gain everything you desire, but lose your soul.

THE PROSPERITY GOSPEL

What good will it be for someone to gain the whole world, yet forfeit their soul?

—Matthew 16:26

The main theme of the gospel isn't being rich in this life, or even being happy all the time. God wants us to be happy, but not in our sin and not at the cost of our character. It is the salvation of man, and the glory of God, that is the theme of the gospel. It isn't a gospel of want, excess, or human will. That is why when we think of God as a prayer-granting genie—as many in the prosperity movement do—we miss the most important part of the model Jesus gave to us. He prayed, "not my will but your will be done," when He was praying to Father God. Prosperity preachers focus on man's will and man's desires, but Jesus focused on the God's will and God's desires.

The Price of the Prosperity Gospel

One of the worst parts of the prosperity message is its aftermath. Because of this belief that God wants everyone to be rich, happy, and healthy all the time, it is impossible to sustain and completely non-Scriptural. It's more than just untrue; it's damaging and dangerous. I have seen firsthand the damage this faulty doctrine brings on people. One reason this is dangerous is that when their life doesn't turn out like the televangelist said it would, one of two things usually happens. Either they think that God has failed them; or they think that they have failed God.

The false version of God they are looking for isn't real, so they never find Him. And when the Lord speaks to them they don't think it is Him. They fail to look for Him in the trial, or the pain, or the test, or the trouble. Because—as these preachers insinuate—if you have enough faith, you should never have any of those things.

Eventually people give up and grow bitter toward God. They think maybe He isn't there. Or if He is there, He just doesn't care.

The other extreme is this. They feel like they are doing something wrong, or they are inferior somehow, when things don't go their way. They assume it is their fault because of a lack of faith. Or that a part of the magic formula for success wasn't implemented correctly. Or maybe it just doesn't work for them. "Maybe something is wrong with me," they say. God always lines up with His Word, so one of the best ways to learn to hear His voice is to know His Word. Commit time to prayer, prayer that is centered around worshiping the Lord, prayer that is centered around seeking Him.

> *I am astonished that you are so quickly deserting the one who called you to live the grace of Christ and are turning to different gospel, which is really no gospel at all. Evidently some people are throwing you into confusion and are trying to pervert the gospel of Christ. But even if we or an angel from heaven should preach a gospel other than the one we preached to you, let them be under God's curse! As we have already said, so now I say again: If anybody is preaching to you a gospel other than what you accepted, let them be under God's curse!*

—Galatians 1:6-10

I believe that the prosperity gospel truly is the "different" gospel Paul talks about in Galatians 1:6. It is dangerous because it causes men to pervert the true gospel of Christ in an effort to justify their greed and sin. One day, every minister, preacher, pastor, teacher, and evangelist will stand before God and give an account for what was preached and taught.

THE PROSPERITY GOSPEL

The prosperity gospel is seductive because it says you can have it all. The road that the prosperity message leads you down is broad and easy, but at its end it leads to destruction. The gospel is not a ladder to financial success; it is not seven steps to a better you. It is the power of sacrifice and the beauty of passion. It's a blood-stained cross and a risen Savior who calls us to lay down our will and our way and follow Him. The road isn't always easy. It's full of tests and trials and self-denial and sacrifice, but in the end, it is the road that leads to life.

> *Enter through the narrow gate. For wide is the gate and broad is the road that leads to destruction, and many enter through it. But small is the gate and narrow the road that leads to life and few find it.*
>
> —Matthew 7:13, 14

CHAPTER 7

THE OFFENSE OF THE CROSS

> All of God's plans have the mark of the cross on them, and all his plans have death to self in them... But men's plans ignore the offense of the cross or despise it. Men's plans have no profound, stern or self immolating denial in them. Their gain is of the world.
>
> —E.M. Bounds

> If the cross is not offensive to man, it is offensive to God.
>
> —Rev. Loren Shreffler

The vision of the cross in the Roman world was offensive. It was meant to be. Its presence on the hillsides, and along the roadways, was meant to strike fear in the hearts of would-be lawbreakers, or revolutionists. Crucifixion on a cross was shameful, painful, long, and agonizing. It was reserved for the worst of society. A Jew being crucified on a cross was especially shameful. This is why the Pharisees wanted Jesus crucified. Yes, they wanted Him dead, but they also thought that the shame of a cross would completely discredit His claim to be the Messiah.

THE OFFENSE OF THE CROSS

> *If someone guilty of a capital offense is put to death and their body is exposed on a pole, you must not leave the body hanging on the pole overnight. Be sure to bury it that same day, because anyone who is hung on a pole is under God's curse. You must not desecrate the land the Lord your God is giving you as an inheritance.*
>
> —Deuteronomy 21:22, 23

But once Christ rose from the dead He settled once and for all that all power and authority belongs to Him. This validated His teachings and that His claim to be equal with God was true. Paul was a Pharisee, and he persecuted the church until he met this resurrected Jesus on the road to Damascus. Because of this meeting, he became a disciple of Jesus and would go on to be the most influential defender of the gospel in history. Paul preached a sharp and bold message, uncompromised, and unashamed. Paul was so changed, and so convinced of the power and truth of the gospel message, that he walked away from everything he had—his social status, political influence, and a comfortable lifestyle—to fully follow the Lord. And then to persuade others to follow the Lord as well. Paul offended people with his message because he never watered it down, or changed it to be politically correct. The truth had gripped him and he would honor it even to the point of his death.

Paul was persecuted because of the gospel. He was abused and mistreated, but he never wavered from the gospel message. All of the apostles, other than John the Revelator, died a martyr's death for preaching the gospel message. The message of the cross is an offense for many reasons, but at its core because it validates the teachings of Jesus. A large part of what Jesus preached was repentance, sin, and final judgement. Jesus was clear that many people would claim to be

Christians without having a valid and real relationship with Him. That is why He spoke these words:

> *Not everyone who says to me, 'Lord, Lord' will enter the kingdom of heaven, but only the one who does the will of my Father who is in heaven. Many will say to me on that day, 'Lord, Lord, did we not prophesy in your name and in your name drive out demons and in your name and perform many miracles? Then I will tell them plainly, 'I never knew you. Away from me, you evildoers!'*
>
> —Matthew 7:21-23

When you truly love someone, and have a deep friendship with them, it doesn't matter if you are persecuted for that friendship. If someone came against your family, you would stand up for your family. Especially if your loved one was in the right in the given situation. Why are some Christians ashamed to tell the truth regarding God's Word? Why do we bow down time and again to the idol of social acceptance and tolerance? Why don't we stand up for our friend, Jesus, and His mission to seek and save the lost? It's because we care more about what people think, or what society thinks, or what our friends think, than we do about what Jesus thinks. We seek the approval of man rather than the approval of God.

Neither Jesus, Paul, nor Peter preached a soft message. They never sought approval from the religious majority, or influential people of their time. If we want to see miracles, and see lives changed, then we have to stop trying to be relevant as defined by the world or the culture of today. We must return to preaching the truth, uncut and powerful. If we edit the truth to be less offensive, we are saying that we are more concerned with the opinion and validation of man, than we are about the mandate of God.

THE OFFENSE OF THE CROSS

The apostle Paul made it clear that salvation was afforded to mankind through grace, and through grace alone. This is offensive to the arrogance of man. Our paper-thin, self-reliance, and our prideful egos, resist this truth. Even in our desperate state, we cling to any shred of self-reliance and dignity we can. This is why the cross is an offense. It says that we are weak, fragile, and dead in our sin. It says the only solution is found in humbling ourselves, and accepting Christ as the only way. It is repenting of our wickedness and accepting the fact that without the cross of Christ we could never be accepted by God. Jesus is the only way. Salvation isn't found in acknowledging that we know Jesus, or that He is one way among many. Salvation is found in acceptance that Christ is the only way to salvation, and that we must repent and turn from the life we once directed. We must submit to Christ and let Him direct our lives. We didn't find Him, He found us.

People who want to grow churches and increase attendance, sometimes try to find ways to present the gospel in a less-than-straight-forward way; in a less-than-honest way. Most people do not want to suffer in any way, even for the truth. They would never be able to stand up to physical persecution. They cannot endure being ridiculed, or verbally mistreated, for Christ sake. Presenting Christ as the only way to God, or saying all things outside of Christ are subject to judgement, will never be on their lips. This is because they do not love God, because they do not know God. To know God, and to be known by God in intimate relationship, is what separates God's children from those who merely play church.

Many people within the church have worked very hard to make the cross friendlier; to make it easier to accept and less offensive. If you take away the offense and the suffering of the cross, you take away the purpose and the power of the cross. Paul preached that unless we die to ourselves we have no place in God's kingdom. Paul taught that if you are unwilling to suffer for the cross, you are not worthy of it, and are an enemy to it.

> *For, as I have often told you before and now tell you again even with tears, many live as enemies of the cross of Christ. Their destiny is destruction, their god is their stomach, and their glory is in their shame. Their mind is set on earthly things. But our citizenship is in heaven. And we eagerly await a Savior from there, the Lord Jesus Christ.*
>
> —Philippians 3:18-20

As people become more and more comfortable, and more and more complacent, as our lives become more and more entrenched in this world and all of its trappings, it seems that we have attempted to build a theology to accommodate that way of life. If your theology doesn't have the cross as its center piece, and your mind is set on earthly things, and your stomach is your god, you are an enemy of the cross. There is no middle ground. People who are eagerly awaiting the return of the Savior are not so interested in planting deep roots in a world that is passing away. We have accepted a false doctrine of pleasure and comfort. Wake up church! Christ is coming back, and He will return for a church without spot or blemish, blood-bought and pure. He will look for a church of people found working and eagerly awaiting His return.

Glory in Suffering

Suffering for something we believe in, or suffering with someone that we love, is a sure sign that we are deeply connected in an intimate way. Yes, God is glorified in our blessing, but the true test

THE OFFENSE OF THE CROSS

of our spiritual character and love and passion for God is when we are persecuted, or go through trials or tests and come out the other side with our faith intact. This is where God shines through.

> *Dear friends, do not be surprised at the fiery ordeal that has come on you to test you, as though something strange were happening to you. But rejoice inasmuch as you participate in the sufferings of Christ, so that you may be overjoyed when his glory is revealed. If you are insulted because of the name of Christ, you are blessed, for the spirit of glory and of God rests on you. If you suffer, it should not be as a murderer or thief or any other kind of criminal, or even as a meddler. However, if you suffer as a Christian, do not be ashamed, but praise God that you bear that name.*
> —1 Peter 4:12-16

God is not sadistic; He does not get pleasure from your pain or your suffering. He is a good and loving God, but that doesn't mean He will never let us endure suffering, because that is not true. Nearly every story in the Bible runs contrary to that train of thought. God is much less interested in your personal comfort than He is in your personal character and your eternal soul. This life is temporary and fleeting—here today and gone tomorrow. It is understandable why people who are only concerned about this life and not the next, try to make this life comfortable at any cost. Because if you live for eighty years, and when you die you cease to exist, then live it up. But for those of us who are in Christ, we should have an eternal perspective. A perspective that reminds us that this present suffering is only for a short time.

> *I consider that our present sufferings are not worth comparing with the glory that will be revealed in us.*

> *For the creation waits in eager expectation for the children of God to be revealed.*
>
> —Romans 8-18, 19

It's not that we should want to suffer, or that serving God is only suffering, but that we shouldn't be surprised when we do suffer. We should be willing, and even grateful, for the opportunity to sacrifice for the cause of the cross, even our lives. God is building His eternal family, and families suffer together, glory together, and stick together during good times and bad. God never said we wouldn't have troubles, or trials, or suffering, or pain. He said that no matter what happens, He would be there in the trial with you, and that He would never leave you or forsake you. God is a God of love, and love endures through good times and bad times.

> *Remember Jesus Christ, raised from the dead, descended from David. This is my gospel, for which I am suffering even to the point of being chained like a criminal. But God's word is not chained. Therefore I endure everything for the sake of the elect, that they too may obtain the salvation that is in Christ Jesus, with eternal glory.*
>
> *Here is a trustworthy saying: If we died with Him, we also live with Him. If we suffer, we will also reign with him. If we disown Him, He will also disown us; If we are faithless, He remains faithful, for he cannot disown Himself.*
>
> —2 Timothy 2:8-13

If we really believe in Christ, that He was raised from the dead, and that He is our only path to salvation, and that one day soon He is coming back, and that all who are outside of Christ are subject to judgement, we would be less concerned about the trappings of this world and more concerned about seeking and saving the lost. When you love someone you are willing to make sacrifices and suffer, especially if you think it will help or benefit the one you love.

Glory always comes at the end of trial or a test. If there's not a trial, then there is no glory. In Scripture, there is always a test or a trial before God's glory is reviled. Take for instance the death and resurrection of Lazarus in John 11. Jesus knew that Lazarus was sick and He could have healed him before he died. In fact, Jesus could have healed him without even going to him—as He did in Luke 7:1-10 with the centurion's servant. But instead, Jesus waited until Lazarus died so that God could be glorified in his resurrection.

A theology without suffering is void of humanity, feeling, and honesty. Suffering sometimes means growing. One of the main objectives of this life is to grow into the image of Christ, and sometimes when you grow, you have growing pains. Jesus' followers saw Him do many miracles, heal the sick, cast out demons, but their minds and hearts still couldn't understand His words. Jesus said in John 14:6 *"I am the way and the truth and the life no one comes to the Father except through me."* Jesus told them that he was *the Life*, but they could not comprehend what He meant until He showed them. The death of Lazarus seemed sad and painful, and to someone without spiritual understanding, probably unnecessary. But in reality, it was a faith-building lesson before God's glory was displayed for all to see.

Suffering, tests, and trials in this life are no different. It is a faith-building, and relationship-building, process by which we grow dependent on God and conform to the image of His Son. This life is short, and those of us who persevere in the faith will see the glory of God in all its power. The point at which we become aware of this truth, is when we are truly at peace and find freedom in whatever circumstance we find ourselves. Eternity-minded people become less concerned with their present sufferings, and more concerned with the future glory of their Savior and Lord Jesus Christ.

> *I know what it is to be in need, and I know what it is to have plenty. I have learned the secret of being content in every situation, whether well fed or hungry, whether living in plenty or in want. I can do all things through Christ who gives me strength.*
>
> —Philippians 4:12, 13

> *Strengthening the disciples and encouraging them to remain true to the faith. "We must go through many hardships to enter the kingdom of God," they said.*
>
> —Acts 14:22

The apostles understood the reality of those hardships, and what Paul meant when he said, *"I can do all things through Christ who gives me strength."* Men do not need strength to endure the good times, full of blessing and prosperity; and men do not suffer and die for causes they don't believe in. Some people of that day may have speculated that Jesus' resurrection was a hoax and didn't really happen. But the men closest to Him, who saw Him in His resurrected body, believed with all of their hearts He was alive. The reality of their witness to Christ's resurrection is sealed by the blood of each one of their martyr's deaths.

Why were they persecuted for speaking the truth of the gospel and preaching the cross of Christ? Because it is offensive to our pride. What the cross represents brings conviction to the heart of a sinful man. They have to discount it as foolishness, because the

THE OFFENSE OF THE CROSS

only other option is to accept it as truth. To do that we have to lay down our life and renounce the throne of our life, and let Jesus have complete authority.

> *For the message of the cross is foolishness to those who are perishing, but to us who are being saved it is the power of God.*
>
> —1 Corinthians 1:18

There is no middle ground. Either the gospel is foolishness or it is the power of God. That is the offense of the cross. That statement leaves no room for compromise. It isn't a modern offense; it is the same offense people have always held. Repentance is offensive to a prideful man. That is why the modern church has minimized it, and some have completely removed it from the way they present salvation. Talking about spirituality and God in a broad and vague way, leaves room for people to live any way they please, which is then accommodated by a theology that is void of repentance.

Jesus wasn't vague; what He preached wasn't vague. He preached *love your neighbor as yourself* and *feed the poor*, but He also preached about repentance and final judgement. There is power in the name of Jesus. His name brings conviction that causes people offense. It is offensive to man's pride and sensibilities to be subject to a God who came in meekness to serve instead of being served. It is offensive to the pride of man that to inherit eternal life he must lay down his life, and his will, and his way. It is offensive to man and secular culture, that if they do not repent of their wickedness and follow Christ, they will be subject to judgement. Salvation is only achieved through the finished work of the cross. We must accept that what Jesus accomplished on the cross, was to pay our debt of sin. Without

Him we could never be restored to God. If you don't like or agree with that message, you are an enemy of the cross.

> *Whoever is not with me is against me, and whoever does not gather with me scatters.*
>
> —Matthew 12:30

Jesus is the only way, and that is the offense of the cross. Paul preached this message. He knew it was offensive but he was out to save souls, not be liked and accepted. They mocked him, ran him out of town, stoned him, and tried to kill him on many occasions. He never changed his message, because he believed in the power of the cross and the importance of its message.

As Christians, we have been entrusted with the most valuable treasure in history, the gospel. There is nothing more important than sharing its truth with the entire world. As true followers of Christ, we should share it carefully and honestly, especially those of us who claim to be preachers, teachers, or evangelists. We will give an account to God one day what we did with our platform, and what we said from behind the pulpit. Not only should our words line up with Scripture, but so should our lives. It is a weighty thing to be responsible for the lives of men and women, but it should be.

> *Not many of you should become teachers, my fellow believers, because you know we who teach will be judged more strictly.*
>
> —James 3:1

We should preach the truth in love. We shouldn't set out to be rude or to offend people, but we should always speak the truth, and proclaim a bold honest gospel. We should be much more concerned with a person's spiritual health than a person's momentary happiness. The postmodern world we live in seems to care less and less about objective truth and basic logic. The stage is set for the light of Christ to be lit and shine brighter than ever before because our world is growing ever darker.

CHAPTER 8

OVERCOMING THE WORLD THROUGH AMAZING GRACE

> Cheap grace is the preaching of forgiveness without requiring repentance, baptism without church discipline, communion without confession, absolution without personal confession. Cheap grace is grace without discipleship, grace without the cross, grace without Jesus Christ.
>
> —Dietrich Bonhoeffer

> I have told you these things, so that in me you may have peace. In this world you will have trouble. But take heart I have overcome the world.
>
> —John 16:33

Jesus truly has overcome the world, which means He has overcome this temporal system corrupted by sin which we were born subject to. We were born into slavery because of an insurmountable debt that we could never pay even if we had a thousand lifetimes to do it. In this book I have tried to explain, through scriptural evidence, that He has overcome the world. I have explained how He overcame the world through the power of the cross, so let's focus a bit on why He overcame the world.

Have you ever considered the fact that God could have destroyed mankind after the fall, and not broken His word or been faithless? One of the most under-preached elements of grace is this. Even if He had not redeemed us, His goodness would still be intact. Justice was demanded by God's standard for the sin of mankind. Sometimes evangelical Christians fail to examine, or attempt to understand, the depth and vastness of God's sovereignty. I say *attempt* because the magnitude of His being and power are exponentially impossible to comprehend. But this doesn't mean we shouldn't try to understand. Unless we have a good concept of God's sovereignty and greatness, we can't ever value and appreciate the gift of grace.

> *For it is by grace you have been saved, through faith-- and this is not from yourselves, it is the gift of God--not by works, so that no one can boast. For we are God's handiwork, created in Christ Jesus to do good works, which God prepared in advance for us to do.*
>
> —Ephesians 2:8-10

As hard as we try to expel pride from our theology, it always reinvents itself and tries to sneak back in. I believe most of us know mentally that our works have nothing to do with our right standing with God. But we know many things on a mental level that somehow never translate to belief deep in our hearts. Knowing something is one thing, but truly believing in your heart brings a sort of a reactionary confidence.

We say that we believe that salvation is by grace and grace alone, but if this is true why do we put so much confidence in ourselves instead of putting our full confidence in Christ. It is because pride is built deeper in us than most of us realize. Pride can blind us, and cause us to fail to understand and value the gift of grace God has given. It is only in humility that we begin to identify, in a more significant way, the greatness of our God, and just how desperate our situation would have been had He not intervened.

People are always debating the question, "Is God good?" They raise questions about Him such as, "If God is good why is there suffering in the world?" Or "If God is good why does He allow pain, death, war, and tragedies?" Although I understand why people ask these questions, the more important question is this: "Is God?" We as humans, especially in America, feel as if we are entitled to an explanation in every situation. But before we start debating whether God is good or not, we should examine if He is real or not. If He is real, and if the Bible is true, then what you *feel* about Him is inconsequential.

Whether you like it or not, you are subject to His authority. God is the sovereign King of all things and the Creator of the universe. He owes us nothing, despite the flawed logic of many in this day and age. We live in an era of entitlement. But make no mistake, God doesn't owe us anything. Once we begin to understand this, and realize we are dead in our sins, only then can we start to grasp the grace of God.

The story of the prodigal son in Luke 15:11-31, is a great example of what it means to come to the place in your life where you finally realize your need for God's grace.

So what is grace? The biblical definition of grace is: *The free and unmerited favor of God, as manifested in the salvation of sinners and the bestowal of blessing.* This is a great definition of grace, but I think there is a better way to explain it. It's sonship! Once we truly understand the extent of our sin debt, and we approach God in repentance for forgiveness of our sins, we go to God seeking mercy.

OVERCOMING THE WORLD THROUGH AMAZING GRACE

But God doesn't give us mercy, instead He gives us grace. What's the difference? Mercy is not getting what you deserve; grace, on the other hand, is getting what you don't deserve. In our case, we ask forgiveness for our sins, and mercy for the judgement we are due. Instead, God wipes away all our sin—past, present, and future. Instead of merely saving us from judgement, He adopts us as sons and daughters, making us part of His eternal family.

> *Jesus continued: "There was a man who had two sons. The younger one said to his father, 'Father, give me share of the estate.' So divided his property between them.*
>
> *Not long after that, the younger son got together all he had and set out for a distant country and there squandered his wealth in wild living. After he had spent everything, there was a severe famine in that whole country, and he began to be in need. So he went and hired himself out to a citizen of that country, who sent him to his fields to feed pigs. He longed to fill his stomach with the pods that the pigs were eating, but no one gave him anything.*
>
> *When he came to his senses, he said, 'How many of his father's hired servants have food to spare, and here I am starving to death! I will set out and go to my father and say to him: Father, I have sinned against heaven and you. I am no longer worthy to be called your son; make me like one of your hired servants.' So he got up and went to his father.*
>
> *"But while he was still a long way off, his father saw him and was filled with compassion for him; he ran to his son, threw his arms around him and kissed him.*

"The son said to him, 'Father I have sinned against heaven and against you. I am no longer worthy to be called your son.'

"But the father said to his servants, 'Quick! Bring the best robe and put it on him. Put a ring on his finger and sandals on his feet. Bring the fattened calf and kill it. Let's have a feast and celebrate. For this son of mine was dead and is alive again; he was lost and is found.' So they began to celebrate.

—Luke 15:11-24

In verse 17 it says, "when he came to his senses." Before the son could ever come seeking mercy from his father, he had to come to his senses. He had to become aware of how he came to be in his present situation—a pigpen. He acknowledged that he had sinned against heaven, but also that he had sinned directly against his father. The son humbled himself and approached the father for mercy.

Yes, life had humbled him, and, yes, his choices had humbled him, but for him to receive grace he had to humble himself and approach the father. The world is full of people who have been humbled and broken by life, by their circumstances, and by their choices. But they refuse to humble themselves and approach God's throne of grace. God will run to you once you make a move toward Him in repentance. God's grace is found in the humility of repentance. Without repentance, there is no grace.

But He gives us more grace. That is why the scripture says: "God opposes the proud but gives grace to the humble."

—James 4:6

God doesn't love us any less when the consequences of our sin humbles us. God loves us so much that He is willing to run to us once we make the slightest movement toward Him. It is impossible to be thankful for something you feel entitled to. Remember, God owes us nothing. Although He owes us nothing He chooses to give us everything. One line that shows the son doesn't understand his sonship is found in Luke 15:21, *The son said to him, "Father, I sinned against heaven and against you. I am no longer worthy to be called your son."* But the son was never worthy to be called his son. He could never earn sonship; he was born into it, just like we are once we are born again. We didn't do anything to earn a place in God's family. He made the way, and all we have to do is accept the place in His family that He offers. We have the ability to choose a slaveship in a foreign land, or sonship in the promised land.

This is what grace is—a place in God's family, forever. We could never overcome the world on our own. We could never overcome and conquer sin on our own. The only real way we can overcome the world is through the grace of God. His grace is sufficient to meet all of our needs. We overcome the world the day we submit our life to God in humility, and begin to live our life for Him. There is no gift greater than the gift of grace. It is only by God's grace that we are forgiven and sealed as His sons and daughters forever.

> *Therefore no one will be declared righteous in God's sight by the works of the law; rather, through the law we become conscious of sin.*
>
> *But now apart from the law the righteousness of God has been made known, to which the Law and the Prophets testify. This righteousness is given through faith in Jesus Christ to all who believe. There is no difference between Jew and Gentile, for all have sinned and fall short of*

the glory of God, and all are justified freely by His grace through the redemption that came by Christ Jesus. God presented Christ as a sacrifice of atonement, through the shedding of His blood--to be received by faith. He did this to demonstrate His righteousness, because in his forbearance He had left the sins committed beforehand unpunished--He did it to demonstrate His righteousness at the present time, so as to be just and the one who justifies those who have faith in Jesus

—Romans 3:20-26

CHAPTER 9

THE CROSS AND EVANGELISM

"We are not diplomats but prophets, and our message is not a compromise but an ultimatum."

—A.W. Tozer

"If we understand what lies ahead for those who do not know Christ, there will be a sense of urgency in our witness."

—David Jeremiah

He said to them "Go into all the world and preach the gospel to all creation. Whoever believes and is baptized will be saved, but whoever does not believe will be condemned."

—Mark 16-15, 16

Without the cross, there is no gospel and without the gospel there is no evangelism. Much of what we call evangelism today, isn't true evangelism at all. We can call it whatever we like, but unless a person is confronted with the fact that they are dead in their sins, and headed towards destruction, and without accepting Christ and living for Him they are lost, we are doing no evangelism.

If someone had cancer and his doctor knew about it, the only ethical thing to do is to explain the graveness of the situation with honesty and care. Then give the patient his or her options. Especially if the doctor knew that with surgery he could cut out the cancer and save the person's life. Yes, the patient will probably be upset by the news, but in order to offer a solution to the problem, you have to be honest about the seriousness of the problem. Getting cut open isn't very appealing, unless you believe that otherwise the cancer could kill you. If left untreated, the cancer of sin is deadly one hundred percent of the time.

Many churches and organizations do outreaches and programs that help people with tough situations and rough times in this life. Outreach programs that build schools, help the poor, feed the hungry, and many other very worthwhile things. These are very important aspects of the church. If we are not helping people, our words don't mean much. But let us never forget these things should be in an effort to share the gospel and to bring glory to Jesus. These things in and of themselves are not enough, we have to boldly preach the gospel.

People in this day and age are much too dignified to preach the gospel wherever they go. Our lives should preach, but so should our words. Words without action are meaningless, but so are actions without words. How will they know you are being helpful in order to glorify God if you don't actually give God the glory? If we don't give God the glory, the glory will be ours by default. We must call on the name of the Lord to be saved, and acknowledge that all glory belongs to Him.

> For, *"Everyone who calls on the name of the Lord will be saved." How, then, can they call on the one they have not believed in? And how can they believe in the*

THE CROSS AND EVANGELISM

> *one of whom they have not heard? And how can they hear without someone preaching to them? And how can anyone preach unless they are sent? As it is written: "How beautiful are the feet of those who bring good news!"*
>
> —Romans 10:13-15

Most people lack the courage or confidence to evangelize people. Even people with whom they have some type of a relationship. Why is this? Many times people will say things like this. "I am just not a talkative person" or "I'm just not built that way." But these same people become very passionate when they are speaking about personal interests that they care about.

The question is this—do we really care about the Lord? Of course anyone who says they are a Christian will say *yes* to this, but if that is true why isn't it coming out of us in our lives and in our conversations? Why isn't sharing our faith the greatest priority of our lives? Do we care about people enough to do everything in our power to share Christ with them and warn them of the coming day of judgement? I believe many will be ashamed about this when they stand before the Lord one day, because they didn't make it more of a priority to share their faith. All we are required to do is share our faith or cast the seed of faith. There's no pressure to make people believe. That is the Holy Spirit's job.

> *I planted the seed, Apollos watered it, but only God has been making it grow. So neither the one who plants nor the one who waters is anything, but only God, who makes things grow. The one who plants and the one who waters have one purpose, and they will each be rewarded according to their own labor. For we are*

> *co-workers in God's service; you are God's field, God's building.*
>
> —1 Corinthians 3:6-9

We are to speak God's word and share our faith wherever we go. That is our part, to plant the seed and to water it. Only God can make things grow. This is what it means when the Scripture says *"The power of life and death is in the tongue."* Our words have the ability to lead people toward salvation. The words of our testimony have life in them. We can plant the seed, or water the seed that leads to eternal life, but only God can make things grow. Only by the drawing of the Lord can anyone know salvation.

> *No one can come to me unless the Father who sent me draws them, and I will raise them up at the last day.*
>
> —John 6:44

We have mission and a mandate from our Lord to seek and save the lost. There is so much talk about our individual purposes in the church today, which is fine to a point. But life isn't about you, about what you can accomplish, or what you can get out of any given situation. Life is about how you can serve God and others. This is one of the greatest lessons of the cross—laying down your life for others. God fills us up so that we can be poured out like a drink offering for the glory of His kingdom. When we're empty, He always fills us up again.

The modern self-centered model of the gospel doesn't leave much room for real evangelism, because our lives are fenced in and self-contained. We have made life so convenient that we have less and less contact with each other. We have all but lost a sense of community as a church. Things people in the church once did to help each other, and bless each other on a regular basis, now is considered a special act of kindness. Blessing someone seems like such a big deal when your life is all about you. It should just be the normal way we live as a part of the community of believers. We feel good about ourselves anytime we have to venture out of our little self-contained comfort zone instead of viewing it as our reasonable Christian service.

What are some of the reasons real evangelism isn't being done in most modern churches?

1. **People don't want to offend anyone.** In the hyper-tolerate world we live in nowadays, it is very unfashionable to speak the truth. Asking someone, "If you died tonight, would you go to heaven?" is considered an invasion of privacy. But to get to heart issues you have to ask heart questions, and most people are unwilling to do that. Not that we should try to offend people, but when it comes down to it, we should care more about their eternal souls than we do about an uncomfortable conversation. If we are truly unashamed of Christ, then we will be willing to speak the truth in love even if it offends someone.

2. **Most people don't know what personal evangelism is.** People think of evangelism as doing an outreach or going on a missions trip. These things can create opportunities for evangelism, but unless the gospel message is presented and proclaimed, no real evangelism is being done. I love subtle ways to reach out to people, and there is a time and a place for everything. But at some point we have to open our mouths and lay out the gospel message. God chose the foolishness of preaching and although this should be done

from the pulpit, the most meaningful evangelism happens one-on-one.

3. **The message of repentance isn't being preached.** Most lost people don't believe that they are lost. A lot of places within the church have stopped dealing with the issue of repentance altogether. Because to have repentance, we have to acknowledge sin, and that doesn't fit in with the feel-good message. There is no gospel without repentance, and without the gospel there is no evangelism. Many people truly believe that their goodness has something to do with their salvation. They believe good people go to heaven, and with that belief there was no reason for Christ to have died on the cross. Logically, there isn't a great need for evangelism to them. When we leave out the need for repentance in our message, we never deal with sin. If sin isn't a problem, then we didn't need a Savior anyway. But the truth is, sin *is* a problem, and one hundred percent of the time it leads to death. That is, unless we repent and surrender to Christ.

4. **We are no longer amazed by amazing grace.** Sometimes it seems we are less than grateful for what Christ has done for us. We have lost our passion. The flame of our first love has died down. We don't talk much about what God has done, or is doing, in our life in a sincere and thankful way. We've gotten used to it, or even worse, we think we deserve it. We expect it because we feel entitled to it. When we consider that the Creator of the universe stepped down from heaven and became a man so that we could be restored to the Father, our hearts should be filled with overwhelming gratitude and thanksgiving. When we consider the lengths God was willing to go to give us the gift of salvation by grace we should be humbled and filled with thanksgiving. When

we truly see that it was by grace alone we were saved, we will be honored to share this gift with other people because we realize it is just that, a gift, that no one deserves. But in His love, God has afforded this gift to all mankind.

5. **We fear rejection more than we fear the Lord.** We are so fragile and delicate, that the idea of being rejected is too much for us to take. The truth is, if we feared the Lord in holiness, it wouldn't matter because we would desire to please God rather than man. The fear of the Lord is almost a lost concept in today's church. Some people believe that because we are His sons and daughters, we no longer owe Him fear, reverence, and respect. In the ancient world, fathers were respected in a much different way than in our modern culture. Obeying the command of our Lord should far outweigh our insecurity and our personal feelings. Fear of the Lord is the beginning of wisdom.

6. **We don't love the lost.** We are judgmental and have no desire to get our hands dirty. Evangelism can be messy and so can ministry. But if we love the lost like Jesus did, we will try to reach them. People are the heart of God. If you don't have love for people in your heart maybe you should check the condition of your heart. Jesus loved the lost so much that He gave His life for them, for us. If we are Christ followers we are also called to give our lives for the lost.

7. **We don't know the lost.** We are in the world and not of the world, but that doesn't mean we should just hide out and wait for Jesus' return. Jesus spent time with and around sinners and lost people. He got to know people by spending time with them. If you want people to hear your words you must build a bridge into their life. It doesn't mean to participate in sin, it means look around in your circle of

influence. Hurting people are all around if you just open your eyes and your heart.

8. **A self-centered gospel.** The focus of so many churches today are aimed at the individual. Your individual success, and your individual purpose, your blessings, and your prosperity, we don't see the need to reach out. The focus is on what we can get rather than what we can give; what we want to gain instead of what we need to let go of. Serving ourselves, instead of serving God and others. We live in a consumer-based society. Unfortunately, that attitude has slipped into the church. Many people think of themselves as customers, and the church as a business that is there to serve them, instead of them being of service to Lord and the church. Customers are not interested in serving others they are there to be served. So the idea of engaging in evangelism doesn't fit into their busy schedules or their important lives.

There is no method or system to evangelism; it is a natural reaction to people's lives being changed. When people's lives are genuinely changed by a Christ-centered gospel you won't be able to stop them from sharing the gift that has been given to them.

If we want revival, God's anointing and power filling our churches once again, we have to take the borders and limits off our churches. We have to stop entertaining, and start worshiping the Lord with passion and reckless abandon, in spirit and truth. We have to stop gauging success by how many people we can fit into our church, and turn control of our church back over to the Holy Spirit. Instead of catering to the whims and wants of men, we need to make the church a house of prayer once again. A place where the holiness of God is reverenced and put above everything else. A place where the cross of Christ and the uncut Word of God is preached from the pulpit. Then true evangelism will be an obvious byproduct.

When men's hearts are truly transformed by the restoration power of Christ Jesus, you won't have to look for evangelism. You won't be able to contain it. True salvation gives birth to passion, and discipleship fans the flame, because things that are on fire catch other things on fire. We must return to prayer, fasting, and seeking the Lord. Only God can bring revival to His people. But God is looking for a hungry and engaged people on whom He can pour out the anointing of His Holy Spirit. Not double-minded, fair-weather Christians, who are so lost in entertaining and pleasing themselves, that the fire of evangelism is far from their hearts.

A Participation Gospel

A consumer gospel is a false gospel. The Gospel of Christ is a participaction gospel and evangelism is an obvious part of this. We are called to be workers, disciples, and evangelists. God chose us and entrusted us with the keys to His kingdom. Churches that are filled with thousands of people who are lukewarm, social, so-called Christians, are not pleasing to God. No matter how much money is raised, no matter how many outreach programs there are, no matter how bright and shiny it is, without real evangelism and the true gospel, it's just another building taking up space. He would rather you be totally lost than lukewarm, comfortable in compromise, and feeling all is well with your soul. At least when you are cold you know you are lacking and in need of something. The Scripture says if you put your hand to the plow and look back, you are not fit for the kingdom of heaven. Evangelism is just an obvious byproduct of the true gospel preached, accepted, and lived out.

I know your deeds, that you are neither cold nor hot. I wish you were either one or the other! So, because you are lukewarm--neither hot nor cold--I am about to spit you out of my mouth. You say, 'I am rich; I have acquired wealth and do not need a thing. But you do not realize that you are wretched, pitiful, poor, blind and naked. I counsel you to buy from me gold refined in the fire, so you can become rich; and white clothes to wear, so you can cover your shameful nakedness; and salve to put on your eyes, so you can see.

—Revelation 3:15-18

We say we don't want to push people away, or cram the gospel down people's throats. I understand that, but let's be honest. Many Christians have made a home in this world, and have become comfortable and complacent. It's time for God's people to rise up in unity and declare in a passionate voice, and an unashamed posture, that Jesus is the only way to salvation. Despite how nice the ship looks on the outside, below the deck it is corrupt and compromised and taking on water. Jesus Christ is the only lifeboat to shore. Do we believe that or don't we? Do we care about the lost or don't we? Are we so comfortable on the ship that we are willing to go down with it? Or if not, are we so selfish that we are walking toward the lifeboat, and not telling others why? The passion with which we move toward salvation, and the way we speak and live, either bears witness to, or denies our convictions.

We have nothing to fear. We have God on our side; we have the truth on our side. If we will be brave and spirit-led, God will empower us to reach the lost just like the apostles did. Remember, God didn't choose the qualified, He equipped the available. And He still does. Evangelism is just a natural expression of someone who has a close friendship with Lord, someone whose passion is so strong that it can't be contained.

If we are in Christ, let us exalt Him. If we are grateful for salvation, let us honor Him with praise. Those who love Him will preach His name, and those who don't will hide behind their pride, and cling to their dignity. Christ is supreme and over all things, and to Him everyone will bow. Some will bow in honor and others in disgrace, but make no mistake, before Him all will bow.

> *Therefore God exalted Him to the highest place and gave Him the name that is above every name, that at the name of Jesus every knee should bow, in heaven and on the earth and under the earth, and every tongue acknowledge that Jesus Christ is Lord, to the glory of God the Father.*
>
> —Philippians 2:9-11